Principles of Business for Caribbean Examinations

Second Edition

Ivan L. Waterman

MACMILLAN
CARIBBEAN

First published 1981
Reprinted 1982 (twice), 1983, 1984 (twice), 1985
Second edition 1986
Reprinted 1987

Published by *Macmillan Publishers Ltd*
London and Basingstoke
*Associated companies and representatives in Accra,
Auckland, Delhi, Dublin, Gaborone, Hamburg, Harare,
Hong Kong, Kuala Lumpur, Lagos, Manzini, Melbourne,
Mexico City, Nairobi, New York, Singapore, Tokyo.*

ISBN 0-333-40910-8

Printed in Hong Kong

British Library Cataloguing in Publication Data
Waterman, Ivan L.
    Principles of business for Caribbean examinations.
    ——2nd Ed.
    1. Commerce
    I. Title
    380.1   HF1007

ISBN 0-333-40910-8

Contents

Preface

'Principles of Business for Caribbean Examinations' is designed to provide a text-book for the Caribbean Examinations Council, Principles of Business section of the Business Education Programme.

The book covers all the material essential for the student. When Principles of Business as a subject was introduced into the school curriculum in 1978, both teachers and students found difficulty in finding material relevant to the Caribbean in one general text. Topics and material were scattered about in a number of brochures, pamphlets and books, and the text-books in use for the subject of Commerce were not always relevant to the West Indian situation. Principles of Business for Caribbean Examinations is an attempt to remedy that situation. The author has attempted to put under one cover all the relevant material needed for teaching the subject in Caribbean schools. It is also hoped that the book will stimulate the minds of students and lead them to further enquiry into the workings and problems of the business world and the economic development of the region in general. The author also wishes to suggest that wherever possible, practical examples be given and that actual research into certain areas of business be conducted so that students develop a true understanding of the world of business.

I.L.W.

Acknowledgements and dedication

The author wishes to thank all those who have contributed in some form or other to the production of this book. Special thanks are owing to the following persons and organisations:

The Personnel Officer   — Plantation Ltd. (B'dos);
The Personnel Officer   — Banks Breweries (B'dos) Ltd;
The Personnel Officer   — The Barbados National Bank;
The Personnel Officer   — Barclays Bank International;
The President   — The Small Business Association (B'dos);
The General Manager   — Pine Hill Dairy Ltd. (B'dos);
The Secretary   — Barbados Chamber of Commerce;
The Secretary   — Barbados Employers' Confederation;
Mr. Malcolm Squires   — Barbados Life Underwriters Association;
Mr. Trevor Hunte   — Barbados Port Authority;
The Barbados Workers' Union and the Caribbean Congress of Labour.

Michael Bourne, for the cover photograph.

C. and R. Korycinski, for their work on the index.

I wish to dedicate this book to my wife, Joan, for her encouragement and love.

1 Introduction

The first inhabitants of the Caribbean were the Caribs and the Arawaks, who lived very simple lives as hunters, fishermen and gatherers of food. Hunting, fishing and food gathering were man's first productive activities. At a later stage in man's development came the planned production of food, which we call farming.

All humans have desires which they would like satisfied. These desires are called wants. Food, clothing and shelter are the basic wants of all people. Further, less urgent, wants are such things as medical care, education and recreation. In order to satisfy these wants man must work. In a simple society he hunts, gathers or fishes. In a more developed society he becomes a farmer, growing crops, or a herdsman, keeping cattle. When man works and produces the things he needs to satisfy his wants we say that he has created utility.

Production, then, is the creation of those goods and services which are capable of satisfying man's wants. By goods we mean those tangible commodities such as food, clothing and houses. Services include intangible things such as entertainment and education. People need services as well as material goods in order to enjoy life to the full.

Let us go back to the early Caribs and Arawaks. At first they were hunters and gatherers. Later they became farmers of a sort, growing small patches of cassava and maize for their own uses. This type of farming is known as subsistence farming, and can still be found in the Caribbean today. Many peasant farmers grow crops and vegetables and keep some animals for the sole purpose of feeding themselves and their families. There is no surplus for trade. This is the simplest form of production, and is sometimes referred to as direct production.

Within each Carib or Arawak village there was another aspect of production going on. The men of a particular family made the bows and arrows, the women made the huts and clothing. Specialisation, the idea of different persons doing different jobs, especially the job which they not only like best, but for which they also have the necessary skill, was very important to the development of trade.

1

In the early stages of specialisation there was tribal specialisation: hunter, fisherman, farmer and herder. For example, while the Egyptians were farmers, the Israelites were herders. This led to a form of trade known as barter: the exchange of goods for goods.

A farmer would exchange corn for wool, or vice versa. This type of trading was good while it lasted, but it was plagued by many drawbacks. First of all there was the problem of deciding on a common value, i.e. how many sheep are worth a bag of wheat. Secondly there was the problem of the 'double incidence of wants'. This means that a person who wanted to barter had first to find someone who had something to exchange for what he wanted and was willing to accept what he had to offer.

| A has corn, wants wool | B has wool, wants fish | C has fish, wants corn |

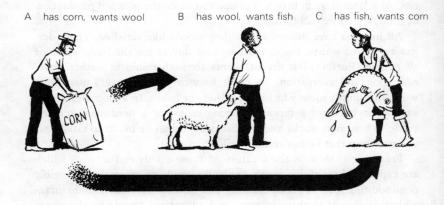

A must first barter with C, then with B

To overcome these drawbacks of barter some common medium of exchange had to be developed. This was necessary for the development and expansion of trade. The problem was solved with the development and use of money.

The introduction of specialisation and of money were essential to the development of modern production and trade. Specialisation led to increased output which meant that there was now a surplus for trade. This increased production was not only the result of simple specialisation (one man doing one job), but was also the result of the division of labour, where a single process of production is further subdivided into a number of simple parts. The result is a vast increase in output per man hour. All modern mass production factories use this principle.

A second benefit of specialisation is that it saves time and tools. Less time is lost when a person can concentrate on one job all the time rather than moving from one job or operation to another. He will only use one or two tools which are used continuously rather than a full set, most of which will lie idle for a good deal of the time.

Specialisation allows a worker to develop his innate ability to the full extent. It also permits a larger amount of standardisation. This is very important to modern industrial production where parts from various sources may be assembled with absolute assurance that any part is exactly the same as any other corresponding one.

Specialisation leads to the development of newer and better methods of production, e.g. inventions, the use of machinery and automation. It allows for easier planning and forecasting, essential features of modern production. Finally, with specialisation we have a new method of production: indirect production, which means that a large number of persons are involved in the production of a particular good or commodity. This leads to increased production with a surplus for trade. When surplus commodities are produced solely for sale in the home market, this is called domestic production.

Farmer   Fisherman   Herder

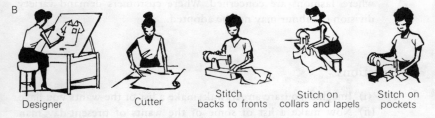

Designer   Cutter   Stitch backs to fronts   Stitch on collars and lapels   Stitch on pockets

(a) Simple division of labour: specialisation by occupation
(b) Complex division of labour in a modern shirt factory: each operation is undertaken by a different person

While specialisation and division of labour are important to the production process, there are limits to the extensive use of them. These limits are of special importance to us in the Caribbean as they tend to influence and affect plans for the industrialisation of the region.

(a) The size of the market is very important. Specialisation leads to increased production and this is desirable only if there exists a sufficiently large demand to absorb the increased quantity of goods on the market. In the Caribbean there may be a case for regional specialisation where each country concentrates on producing those goods for which it has the greatest advantage in production. Also, industries could be farmed out to countries, to prevent duplication and undue competition.

(b) In the Caribbean area we are entering into the field of industrialisation at a late stage. In most of our countries labour is plentiful and the economy as a whole is poor, so there is really no reason to economise on labour by employing the process of division of labour. It is only when the demand for the services of labour increases that division of labour becomes really practicable.

(c) The nature of production is another limit to specialisation and division of labour. Division of labour is feasible only if the production process can be split up into separate stages. Where such splitting up is impossible, division of labour has no place. Thus division of labour is more suitable to manufacturing industry than to agriculture which is still the mainstay of many island economies. Generally, division of labour requires a large organisation which must be kept fully employed. It is a waste of time and money to build up a large organisation if such an organisation is only going to operate part-time.

(d) Specialisation necessitates standardisation of the product. In some trades and industries this is considered undesirable, especially where fashions are concerned. Where customers demand variety, division of labour may not be adopted.

Questions

1   (i) Imagine you are an Arawak; make a list of the wants you have.
    (ii) Now make a list of some of the wants of present-day man. How do they compare?

2   Define (a) domestic production, (b) subsistence production (c) indirect production. Give examples of each type of production.

3 What do you understand by the term specialisation? Show how specialisation has (i) led to different occupations; (ii) benefited production.
4 Draw up a list of industries and show how regional specialisation can take place in the Caribbean.
5 What are the major shortcomings of a barter system? How can money correct these shortcomings?

2   Production

In Chapter 1 we saw that humans have wants which must be satisfied and that in order to satisfy those wants they must produce suitable goods and services. This chapter will examine production.

First let us distinguish between goods and services. In Chapter 1 we saw that goods are tangible commodities which satisfy human wants and that services are intangible things which also have the power to satisfy human wants, e.g. food is a good; education is a service.

In our modern economy we can classify goods as either consumer goods or producer goods, and we can further subdivide these into single use goods or durables.

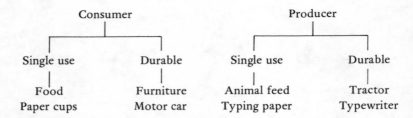

Types of goods

This diagram shows a very important point to be borne in mind when deciding whether a good is a consumer good or a producer good, and that is the question of use. Returning to the diagram, a typewriter can be a consumer good as well as a producer good, so, too, can a motor car, e.g. a company car, or paper cups issued to workers in a canteen. It all depends on the use to which the good is put. Services too can be classified. We have commercial services and direct services. Direct services are productive in themselves as they satisfy wants directly, e.g. the dentist who extracts an aching tooth. Commercial services assist production by adding utility to a good, e.g. transportation of products from factory to retailer.

Direct	Commercial
Doctor	Wholesaler
Dentist	Banker
Teacher	Transport driver
Policeman	Merchants

Services

Having distinguished between goods and services, let us now look at production. Goods and services are needed to satisfy wants, but before these wants can be satisfied the goods and services must be produced. The question is how, and with what are we going to produce those goods and services, and how much are we going to produce?

In order to produce we need natural resources and human effort. The quantity produced depends on the quantity and quality of natural resources available and the amount of human effort exerted.

Factors of production

In order for production to take place two or more of the following factors must be present.

(a) Natural resources, or 'land' as they are called in economics. These include soil, water, forest, minerals, etc.

(b) Capital in the form of machines, plant, etc. Capital is the result of past human effort.

(c) Labour: manual or mental. This is the human endeavour.

(d) Organisation or enterprise. This refers to the organising, coordinating or combining of land, labour and capital, in order to produce. The person who takes the risk of enterprise is called the entrepreneur.

NATURAL RESOURCES
Here are some of the natural resources found in the Caribbean. We may classify them as renewable and non-renewable resources.

Renewable resources are those which are replaced either by natural processes, or by the efforts of man. Non-renewable resources are those which cannot be replaced.

Natural resources are very important to production for, as was said earlier, the level of production in a country is determined by the quantity

7

Renewable	Non-renewable
Fertile land	Oil
(renewable by reclamation and	Pitch
use of fertilisers)	Bauxite
Fish (by scientific fish farming)	Gypsum
Forest (by refforestation)	
Water (by nature)	
Wind (by nature)	
Sunshine	

Resources

and quality of the natural resources available. In Chapter 4 we shall see that natural resources determine the type of industry found in the country.

Land ownership
The traditional pattern of land ownership in the Caribbean may be classified as follows:
(a) Crown Lands — owned by Government.
(b) Plantations — owned by (i) foreign companies, (ii) private families and individuals, (iii) limited liability companies and partnerships.
(c) Peasant holdings — owned by small farmers.

The most productive lands were generally owned or controlled by large foreign (multinational) companies e.g. Tate and Lyle, Texaco, Alco. Thus Tate and Lyle, and Caroni Ltd., at one time owned and controlled large areas of Jamaica and Trinidad. This domination of productive land by foreign companies has, to some extent, been broken in recent years. The Governments of Guyana, Trinidad and Jamaica have been nationalising or purchasing numbers of these foreign interests, thus changing the pattern of land ownership. We still, however, have a large number of plantations owned by a few families, limited companies or partnerships. In some countries as much as 85% of the land is owned by these plantations, the remaining 15% being owned by a large number of small farmers.

LABOUR
Labour is considered by many economists as the fundamental agent of production; they argue that there can be no production without some kind of labour, whether it be manual, i.e. working with the hands, e.g. lifting, carrying, cutting, or mental, i.e. working with the brain, e.g. managing, trading, accounting, being a doctor. However the same

8

argument holds good for natural resources.

Labour may be classified as

(a) skilled: having a special ability to do a particular job. Skills may be acquired by training or experience.
(b) unskilled: having no special ability.
(c) semi-skilled: a particular ability is only partially developed.

More and more, however, labour is tending to become highly specialised.

The supply of labour

The labour force may be defined as all those persons who are either employed, or are looking for employment. In the Caribbean territories it is generally acknowledged that the labour supply far outnumbers the jobs available, and that it consists mainly of unskilled agricultural workers. However, as educational facilities become increasingly available, we find a large number of the unemployed consists of young people who are looking for white collar jobs as opposed to work in the agricultural sector.

Factors which affect the labour supply

The supply of labour at any one time is determined by (i) the size of the population; (ii) the age-distribution of the population; (iii) social habits, with special regard to whether married women go out to work or stay at home; (iv) the compulsory school-leaving and retirement age and whether or not retired persons are allowed to work.

The productivity of labour is also affected by its efficiency. There are several important factors which determine the efficiency of labour.

(a) The level of education of the worker. Education determines the trainability of workers and the development of the skill of workers. Skill in today's world of industry may mean the worker's ability to handle tools and machinery, separating education and training. Training 'on the job' is often far more significant than the worker's educational level.
(b) The standard of health of the workers. If workers are not in the best of health they cannot produce efficiently and output will drop considerably.
(c) Proper organisation. This is essential if labour is to be efficient. Good organisation ensures that square pegs are not put in round holes and that workers are given the correct tools with which to work.
(d) Working conditions. The layout and conditions of the factories must be such that the workers enjoy the best working conditions.
(e) Wages, both their level and the system of payment. High wages can lead to a more efficient labour force since it will be not only healthier but also stronger and less likely to be absent. A system of

paying by piece rates can raise productivity.
(f) The degree of specialisation. Labour is less likely to be unemployed if it is mobile both occupationally and geographically.

CAPITAL

Capital as a factor of production means those goods which have resulted from past efforts, and which have been set aside to increase or improve further production. For example, when a farmer stores seeds from the present crop to plant at a later date, the seeds are capital. The tools in a repair shop are capital, so too is machinery.

The functions of capital

(a) To make labour more productive, e.g. by using machinery, tools, plant.
(b) To assist in specialisation and the division of labour. Stock of goods can be stored for future consumption.
(c) To assist man in performing jobs which would normally be beyond his capacity as a human. Thus engines such as cranes, steam hammers and power drills are used to carry out certain operations.
(d) To produce commodities ahead of demand, thus production anticipates demand and an entrepreneur can undertake experiments and research, as well as the risk of production.

ENTERPRISE OR ORGANISATION

By now it should be fairly obvious that even the simplest form of production calls for some coordination between the factors of production. Enterprise or organisation is responsible for the direction and control of production. The organiser or entrepreneur coordinates and organises the other factors of production and undertakes the risks of anticipating demand ahead of actual consumption.

Organisation is not simply a special branch of labour, for it calls for and requires qualities distinct from those required for any other branch of labour. There is also the very important fact that you cannot hire a man to invest his money and take the risk of production. The entrepreneur is the man (or group of persons in case of big business) who does the anticipating and starting of production. It is he who maintains, organises and manages the production as it grows and becomes more complex.

The functions of the entrepreneur

(a) To initiate production.
(b) To bring together the necessary resources of land, labour and capital.
(c) To organise those resources in the correct proportions.

(d) To employ them, and pay them for the work they do.

(e) To bear the risks (non-insurable) of (i) production in anticipation of demand; (ii) loss through bad management.

(f) To provide the finance needed before production can take place.

The entrepreneur's major risk is that what he produces may not sell at all, or that he may have to sell it at a price which would prevent him from covering his cost of production. Any financial gain or loss is his.

Some people believe that entrepreneurs are born; others believe that with training one can become a good entrepreneur. Whatever the case, it is known that in the Caribbean we need people with this kind of skill if we are to succeed in our industrialisation thrust, if we are to be less dependent on foreign entrepreneurs and investors who must be allowed tax holidays and the right to repatriate their profits, and if we are to become more self reliant.

Finally, the above analysis assumes that the entrepreneur is an individual, and to some extent the assumption is true in the Caribbean. However, in the world of modern business with large limited liability companies, the one-man entrepreneur has been displaced in many areas of industry. The modern joint stock companies function through shareholders' meetings, and the board of directors and the managing director. The shareholders make profits or losses when managerial decisions prove to be right or wrong, and thus the shareholders perform the risk-bearing functions. They, however, do not make price-output decisions. These decisions are made by the manager and his advisers who may or may not be shareholders. There is therefore no automatic connection between the entrepreneurs' price-output decisions and the risk-bearing function in the modern world of business.

Questions

1 What do you understand by the terms: (i) goods and services; (ii) consumer and producer goods.

2 Distinguish between renewable and non-renewable resources. Give examples of each.

3 What are the factors of production? Can production take place without any one of these factors?

4 What factor affects the supply and efficiency of labour?

5 Which of the following is an entrepreneur: (i) sole trader; (ii) an ordinary shareholder in a company? Explain your answer.

11

3 Classification of production

We now know why production takes place, i.e. to satisfy human wants. We also know the difference between goods and services and the factors that must be present if production is to take place. Let us now examine the different types of production.

Branches of production

The chart on page 13 shows that production has three main areas or divisions: (i) industry; (ii) commerce; (iii) direct services. Industry deals with the collection of the natural resources in their raw state and the conversion of these to actual goods. In short, industry deals with production *per se*. Commerce deals with the distribution and exchange of the goods produced: trade and aids to trade. Services are divided into two sub-divisions: those services which are themselves productive, and those which assist the process of production and distribution. In practice, we distinguish three types of production: (i) primary; (ii) secondary; (iii) tertiary.

Primary	Secondary	Tertiary
Extractive industry	Manufacturing	Services
Agriculture	Construction	(Direct and
Fishing		commercial)
Mining		

Types of production

Primary production involves the gathering or harvesting of crops, e.g. sugar cane, or the extracting of resources from the land or sea, e.g. mining of bauxite.

Secondary production involves the changing of form of the raw

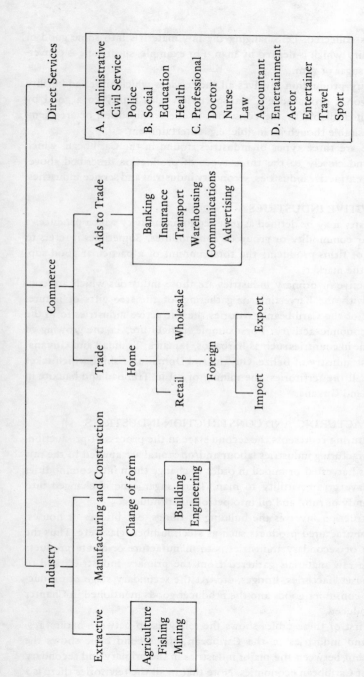

Branches of production

materials collected, i.e. changing the raw materials into some good or commodity which is desired by man. For example, sugar cane is converted into sugar or rum.

Tertiary production involves all the services which either add utility to the goods produced e.g. transportation adds utility to a good by making it available to the consumer in the retail outlet, or are themselves desirable though intangible, e.g. entertainment.

There are three types of industries, found in the Caribbean, which correspond closely to the three types of production described above; they are extractive industries, secondary industries and service industries.

EXTRACTIVE INDUSTRIES
An industry may be defined as that economic activity which produces a particular commodity or group of commodities. Sometimes it refers to a group of firms producing the total amount of a particular good supplied to the market.

Extractive or primary industries are those industries which are concerned with the harvesting, or gathering, of the free gifts of nature. In many of the Caribbean territories the extractive industries form the major economic activity. For example, agriculture, or the growing of sugar cane in countries such as Barbados, Jamaica, Trinidad and Guyana; the forest industry of Belize, Guyana and Dominica; fishing which takes place in all the territories; the mining of oil in Trinidad and bauxite in Jamaica and Guyana.

MANUFACTURING AND CONSTRUCTION INDUSTRIES
Manufacturing represents the second stage in the process of production. In manufacturing industries labour and/or capital are applied to the raw materials harvested or mined in order to change them into commodities which have greater utility to man. Thus, sugar cane is changed into sugar, candy or rum, and oil into petroleum products.

Construction involves the building of things, e.g. bridges or houses, using manufactured products such as steel, lumber, glass, etc. Thus the function of secondary industries is to manufacture or create products from the raw materials gathered from the primary industries, and to build houses, factories, bridges, etc. At the secondary stage of production the consumer goods and the producer goods mentioned in Chapter 2 are produced.

The first of these tables shows the relationship between natural resources and industries in the Caribbean; the second table shows the relationship between the major industries in the primary and secondary sectors of Caribbean economies. Note that in all the territories there is a strong connection between the natural resources, the industries in the primary sector and those in the secondary sector. Most of the industries at the primary level are labour intensive with low technological demands.

Natural resources	Industries
Land (arable and grazing)	Agricultural, agro-industries e.g. food processing
Bauxite	Alumina
Oil	Petroleum products, fertilisers, paints
Pitch	Asphalt
Sea	Salt
Sun	Solar energy, tourism
Wind	Unexploited
Forest	Furniture, lumber, balata, chewing gum
Gypsum	Plaster of Paris, cement
Tin	Unexploited

Natural resources and industries

SERVICE INDUSTRIES

Service industries are of two kinds: commercial services, e.g. banking and insurance, and direct services, e.g. entertainment, tourism. Commercial services act as aids to production, while direct services are intangible productive services.

Let us take transportation as an example of a service industry. Transportation, which is the movement of goods and passengers from one place to another, plays a very important part in the production process. It brings the final product to the consumer in the right place at the right time. In other words, it helps to complete the production process.

There is also another aspect to transportation. It satisfies the desire of the travelling public for some means of swift and comfortable travel, and it also satisfies their desire to see places outside their immediate environment or home.

Country	Primary	Secondary
Barbados	Agriculture, sugar cane, mining of oil	Rum, milk, garments, furniture, electronics, processed foods
Guyana	Agriculture, mining of bauxite, forestry, growing of rice, sugar cane	Rum, processed foods, garments
Jamaica	Agriculture, mining of bauxite, citrus, sugar cane, bananas	Rum, processed foods, garments, soap, leather, cement, other light manufacturing
Trinidad	Mining oil, pitch, agriculture, sugar cane, citrus	Asphalt, petrochemicals, motor-car assembly, fertilisers, rum, soap, other light manufacturing
Windward Islands	Bananas, citrus, cocoa, spices, arrowroot, cotton	Canned juices, cartons, rum, flour, edible oil, soap, lime oil, straw goods
Leeward Islands	Limes, cotton, vegetables	Rum, oil refining, garments, furniture, gin, soap, cooking oil

Major industries found in the Caribbean by territories

Communication and advertising are two service industries which are important to the world of business. In our modern economies production is organised ahead of demand and so contracts must be made with agents and wholesalers in advance. The buying public must be stimulated by publicity and advertising. Thus, adequate means of communicating must exist, and advertising is necessary for securing sales. Another service industry which is important to many Caribbean countries is the

Production chain (opposite page)

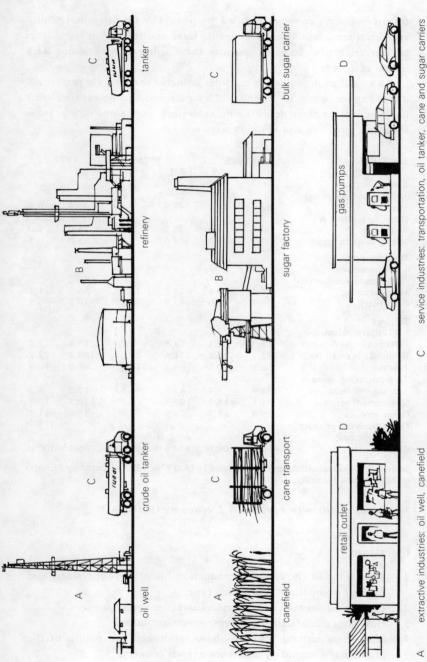

oil well   crude oil tanker   refinery   tanker

canefield   cane transport   sugar factory   bulk sugar carrier

retail outlet   gas pumps

A   extractive industries: oil well, canefield   C   service industries: transportation, oil tanker, cane and sugar carriers

B   secondary industries: oil refinery, sugar factory   D   retail outlets: shop, gas pump

tourist industry, commonly called tourism. The tourist industry provides accommodation, entertainment, food and recreation for visitors to our countries. Tourism provides the Caribbean with about $1.5 billion each year.

As a final example, let us consider a doctor's service. He performs a direct service when he attends to his patients, and he satisfies their health needs or their desire to be made well from some illness. He is therefore providing a production service.

SECTOR	1975		1976		1977	
	$M	%	$M	%	$M	%
Extractive						
(Primary industries)						
Sugar	95.0	14.5	44.9	6.6	49.4	6.5
Other agriculture &						
fishing	30.4	4.6	36.5	5.4	38.0	5.0
Mining & quarrying	2.2	0.3	3.6	0.5	4.0	0.5
Manufacturing &						
Construction						
(Secondary industries)						
Manufacturing	69.4	10.6	78.2	11.6	86.8	11.4
Construction	36.9	5.6	43.9	6.5	49.2	6.5
Services						
(Tertiary industries)						
Electricity, gas & water	13.9	2.1	14.5	2.2	16.5	2.2
Wholesale & retail trade	132.2	20.1	151.6	22.5	180.3	23.7
Tourism	66.5	10.1	69.2	10.3	83.0	10.9
Transportation, storage						
& communications	38.9	5.9	43.5	6.5	47.2	6.2
Government services	94.1	14.3	109.7	16.3	120.7	15.9
Other services	76.8	11.7	78.9	11.7	85.0	11.2
Gross domestic product						
at factor cost						
Costs	656.1	100.0	674.6	100.0	760.1	100.0

Source: Provisional estimates for Barbados 1975, 1976, 1977 prepared by Ministry of Finance and Planning.

Sector contribution to a typical W.I. economy (Barbados)

Questions

1 Make a list of the types of production found in your country and list four occupations under each type.
2 Distinguish between direct services and commercial services.
3 How does manufacturing differ from construction?
4 Show how natural resources have influenced the nature of the primary and secondary industries in your country.

4 Economic systems

Economics can be defined as the study of scarcity and choice. It is because resources are scarce relative to man's wants that all countries experience an economic problem.

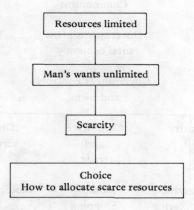

The economic problem

This diagram shows the economic problem which countries face in the developing Caribbean countries. Our resources are limited, but the wants of our people are unlimited. We are therefore faced with the problem of how to allocate our scarce or limited resources among competing wants. This brings us to the problem of choice: choosing the right use or combination of uses that would ensure the satisfaction of as many wants as possible, or, as the economist would say, the problem of how best to maximise satisfaction.

All countries are faced with this basic economic problem and any economic system must answer the questions:

(a) What is to be produced?
(b) How much is to be produced?
(c) How is it to be produced?
(d) Where is it to be produced?
(e) How are the factors of production to be rewarded?

Economic systems differ in their approach to the basic economic problem and in the methods employed to solve the above questions. Three main approaches or systems have been developed to solve the economic problem. These systems are (i) collectivism, which includes communism, socialism and cooperative republics, i.e. planned economies; (ii) capitalism in which we include *laissez-faire*, private enterprise, and an uncontrolled economy; (iii) mixed economies.

Collectivism

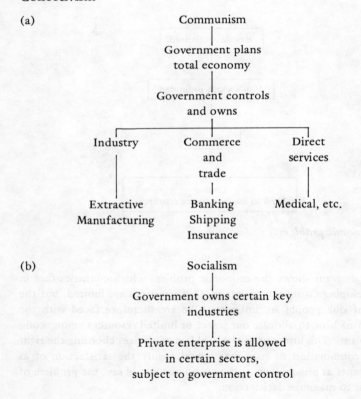

(a)

Communism
|
Government plans
total economy
|
Government controls
and owns

Industry   Commerce   Direct
                and   services
                trade

Extractive   Banking   Medical, etc.
Manufacturing   Shipping
                Insurance

(b)

Socialism
|
Government owns certain key
industries
|
Private enterprise is allowed
in certain sectors,
subject to government control

Organisation of planned economies

Under the communist system as practised in the USSR the state owns and controls the means of production (factories, farms, mines, forests, etc.) and keeps the profit from these industries, to be used for the benefit of all the people in the country. The state appoints all managers to factories and farms. It dictates the crops to be grown on each farm and the production targets to be attained. Similar targets are set for workers in factories and mines. Also, all prices and wages are set by the state.

ADVANTAGES OF SUCH A SYSTEM

(a) Government can decide what needs to be produced for the good of the country as a whole, and direct resources into those areas.

(b) Profits resulting from industry and agriculture can be used (i) to buy more capital equipment and so to increase production; (ii) to build more hospitals and schools and provide better welfare services; (iii) so that workers can be paid higher wages.

(c) No group of workers can force up their wages by striking or by putting up prices, since the state controls all wages and prices.

(d) Workers may be prepared to work harder since they may feel that they are working for themselves and for their country.

(e) Incomes are evenly distributed.

DISADVANTAGES

(a) Estimating just how much of a commodity is needed by the whole economy at a particular time is a difficult task, since the planners may not have correct estimates about demand, and since they cannot estimate for unforeseen conditions.

(b) Managers who have no financial interest in a firm may lack the incentive to work. However, in a communist system managers who are unproductive are fired or demoted and so they would usually give of their best.

(c) Central planning calls for a lot of personnel which in itself may mean a wastage of manpower.

(d) What the country needs may not be the same thing as what the people in the country want. The planners may think the country needs roads and houses while the people want consumer goods, especially luxury items.

In some communist countries, e.g. Yugoslavia, an attempt has been made to give the workers more say in the running of the enterprises where they are employed. Workers' councils have been set up and decisions on production, investment, wages and marketing are made by the councils.

21

Capitalism

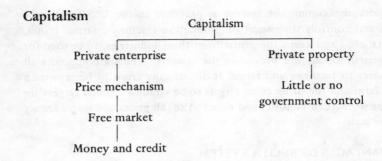

```
                        Capitalism
                            |
     ┌──────────────────────┴──────────────────────┐
Private enterprise                          Private property
     |                                             |
Price mechanism                             Little or no
     |                                      government control
Free market
     |
Money and credit
```

Market-orientated economy

In a capitalist economy production is organised so that the capital equipment is bought and owned by individuals who then pay workers to come and operate the machinery. Emphasis is laid on the freedom of the individual, both as a consumer and as the owner of a factor or factors of production.

An individual can work where he wants, while entrepreneurs are also free to set up enterprises of their own choosing. Private individuals are the owners of the means of production (mines, forests, farms, etc.) and, in theory, it is they who decide what to produce, in what quantities, how it is going to be produced, the price of the finished goods, the rewards of labour, etc.

In a capitalist system these important decisions are not made by the entrepreneurs alone, but by the price mechanism. Consumers make their choice or preferences known in the free market by registering their demand for a particular product. Demand is made by their willingness and ability to pay the going price for a particular commodity. Producers would then produce those goods for which there is the greatest demand. Thus, the price mechanism or system is an essential part of the capitalist system, as it is through this mechanism that decisions are made about the allocation of scarce resources.

ADVANTAGES

(a) Individuals have freedom of choice.

(b) People are free to work wherever they choose.

(c) Wants can be easily gauged. Changes in wants are reflected by changes in the price system.

(d) Efficiency is achieved as a result of profit incentive.

(e) Because owners wish to obtain the greatest possible return from their factors of production, they take these factors to where the return is highest. Thus, production responds to changes in demand, leading to an optimum allocation of resources.

(f) The price system registers wants and arranges the allocation of factors of production automatically. It operates without a host of officials.

DISADVANTAGES

(a) It leads to great inequalities of wealth, for the rule 'To him that hath more shall be given', seems to apply fairly generally in the accumulation of wealth.

(b) Since profit is the dominant motive, only those goods which yield the highest profits would be produced.

(c) If left entirely to private enterprise some goods and services would not be produced at all or would be produced so inefficiently that the total supplied would be quite inadequate.

(d) Certain forms of competition may themselves lead to waste and inefficiency in the use of the factors of production.

(e) In practice the competition upon which the efficiency of the capitalist system depends may disappear.

(f) The motive of private profit does not ensure that public welfare, as distinct from private welfare, will be maximised.

(g) Under capitalism there occur periods when factors of production are allowed to stand idle because producers as a whole consider that the prospects of making a profit are poor.

Mixed economies

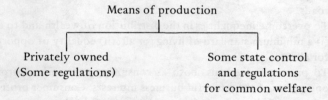

Means of production

Privately owned
(Some regulations)

Some state control
and regulations
for common welfare

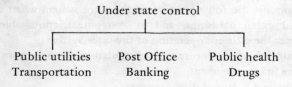

Under state control

Public utilities
Transportation

Post Office
Banking

Public health
Drugs

Organisation of mixed economies

23

In most Caribbean countries the economic system is neither purely capitalist nor is it communist. Much of industry is in the hands of privately owned companies, while some organisations are owned and controlled by the state. Ownership of most of the means of production of goods and services is in the hands of private individuals organised into business firms. Some governments control water, electric power, publications, transportation and mines. There is also some government action to encourage parts of the economic process by means of tariffs, subsidies and patents. Some government activity also discourages certain activities for reasons of health and safety. Government intervention has actually increased in recent years.

Governments intervene either by (i) nationalising certain industries, or (ii) regulating the policies of certain industries.

REASONS FOR NATIONALISATION AND REGULATIONS

(a) To increase efficiency, e.g. nationalisation of transportation. This is brought about by the reorganisation and recapitalisation of the industry.

(b) To keep some industries going for the sake of the whole economy, e.g. to provide some service considered to be essential to the public. This may simply be to provide employment.

(c) To facilitate overall planning for the whole economy. Certain industries are nationalised or regulated so that government could better plan for the whole economy and not just for a few sectors.

(d) To produce goods and services which would either not be provided by private enterprise or might be provided very indifferently, e.g. roads.

(e) To overcome inequalities in the distribution of wealth and to ensure (i) a minimum standard of living for all; (ii) equality of opportunity for all.

(f) To protect individuals, both as consumers and workers, from the operations of the powerful business interests. Consumer protection, price controls and regulating of wages and labour practices are examples.

(g) To modify the full operation of the price system when shortages would entail hardships, and to overcome friction which might hamper the efficient operation of the price system.

(h) To control entrepreneurs and to regulate the economy in order to secure full employment.

(i) To obtain a balanced development.

(j) To maintain a stable level of prices.

(k) To ensure a sturdy growth of national production.
(l) To improve the balance of payments in order that foreign currency reserves may be strengthened.

Questions

1 Most Caribbean governments claim to be 'Democratic Socialists'. What type of economy would you expect to find in such countries?
2 Compare and contrast the collectivist system with the capitalist system.

5 Industry

In Chapter 3 we examined the branches of production and we saw that industry was one of the three branches of production, the others being commerce and services. In that chapter we also saw that industry is related to the types of production; e.g. extractive industries are related to primary production, manufacturing and constructing industries are related to secondary production and service industries are related to tertiary production. We also defined an industry as the economic activity which produces a particular commodity or group of commodities.

We may further define industry in the broader sense as all the economic activities which have to do with the extracting or gathering of natural resources, the manufacturing of these resources into goods to satisfy human wants and the provision of services either to further complete production or to directly satisfy a want.

In this chapter we shall examine the relationship between natural resources and cottage industries and linkage industries.

Cottage industries or handicrafts

Cottage industries are industries carried on in the home. Handicraft is some skilled occupation or work, done by hand. Putting the two together, we see that cottage industries are skilled occupations, e.g. making of souvenirs, shell and coconut craft, handwork such as knitting, smocking and other art forms done manually (by hand), by craftsmen, in their homes.

The word 'manufacture' actually means 'making with the hands', and dates back to the period when many of the items which are now made by machinery in factories were actually made by hand in homes or cottages (cottage industry).

Cottage industry, or handicraft, as it is called today, was the earliest form of manufacture. If we go back to our early Caribs and Arawaks, we find that items such as hammocks, moccasins and blankets were made by hand by the women of the village. The earliest settlers too made a number of the items, such as furniture, which they needed.

RESOURCES AND COTTAGE INDUSTRIES

In the Caribbean we are fortunate in that there are a number of natural materials which could form the basis of cottage industries. We have an abundance of sand and sea shells, calabash seeds and beads, fibres (bamboo and straw), various woods, coconut shells, fruits (preserves), to name a few. We also have various discarded items such as bottles, plastic cups, match-sticks and boxes, pallet sticks and other items which could be utilised by industrious individuals to make objects.

The development of cottage industries could be an important tool in national development strategies. Cottage industry provides a source of self employment and income to many. It helps to cut down on the importation of such items as fruitware and souvenirs, and can become a major source of earning foreign currency (a) by means of direct export to other countries, and (b) indirectly when goods are sold to tourists.

With the development of tourism in many territories, the opportunities for the development of cottage industries have increased. Many governments have assisted in the development of cottage industries by providing training in handicraft for those who want it, e.g. training in pottery, batik work, leather craft, etc. Some governments have even provided marketing facilities for those engaged in cottage industries, and factory space and small loans for those who want to expand. The future could be a bright one for the development of cottage industries in the region.

Linkages between industries

We have seen that there are three types of productive industries,
1 **Extractive,** e.g. agriculture and mining.
2 **Manufacturing,** e.g. food processing and petro-chemicals.
3 **Service,** e.g. transportation and tourism.

The question of linkages between these sectors is of crucial importance in the process of Caribbean development. The primary produce requires some kind of product elaboration before reaching the consumer, e.g. farm products have to be graded, sorted, processed, packaged, stored and transported before final consumption. As demand for these services increases, intermediate institutions specialising in their production emerge and many activities previously performed on farms are transferred to non-farming enterprises. As the commercialisation of agriculture increases and as technology improves, there is an increased

27

demand for off-farm inputs such as artificial fertilisers, animal feeds of various kinds, farm equipment and building materials. Thus a series of relationships develops between the productive sectors, where the product of one industry becomes the raw material for another and the services sector provides the links which hold them together.

Rearing of livestock

Primary production	Secondary production	Service	Type of linkage
Meat	Meat processing: corned beef, curry mutton	Raw material and finished goods to be transported. Secretarial and commercial services; retail outlets.	Forward Forward
Milk	Dairy products: butter, cheese, yogurt		Forward Forward
Hides	Leather tanning and bones; shoes, bags, belts, meal		Forward Forward
	Feed processing for animals; Building materials and farm implements, dairy equipment.		Backward Backward Backward Backward

Linkages in agricultural production

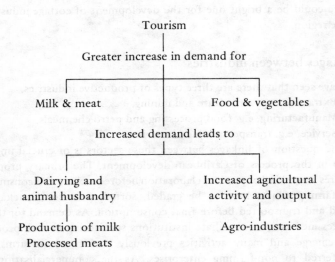

Impact of tourism as a creator of linkages

Linkage industries, or industries which are related in such a way that the products of one become the raw materials of the other (forward linkage) at the same time as the demands of one lead to the establishment of the other (backward linkages), are very important as they lead to increases in output, income, and employment. Given the high level of unemployment in our economies, the creation of linkage industries could help to overcome some of our major problems.

In almost all of the territories, agriculture forms the economic base. In at least three there are mineral deposits in the form of oil, pitch and bauxite, and forests can still be found in many. Agriculture can form the basis of an important agro-industrial drive in many countries and the development of linkage industries. Crops such as vegetables, yams, potatoes, cassava and corn can be preserved, dehydrated or canned. Animal feeds and fertilisers can be manufactured locally for use in the local livestock industry. We can have regional linkage industries where the raw materials in some countries are manufactured in others for use by all and we can have local linkage industries. Oil and pitch form the basis of a petro-chemical industry in Trinidad. Local forest trees are used in some countries in their building and furniture industries. Bauxite is yet to be used as the basis for local industries. Cottage industries may develop which may lead to the formation of more linkage industries. The major drawback or hindrance to the development of linkages using locally based products is capital. In all of the territories capital is very scarce, hence industrialisation in the region has been by invitation.

Implications of mechanisation and automation

In the Caribbean we are faced with a dilemma. We need to modernise our industries, to keep pace with other industrialised or industrialising countries; on the other hand we are faced with a large, mainly unskilled labour force and massive unemployment. The question is how do we resolve this dilemma? Maybe you, as students, could come up with suggestions.

There are many benefits to be derived from the introduction of mechanisation and automation in our drive to become industrialised. At present our rate of productivity is relatively low. Mechanisation could increase productivity and total output, at the same time reducing the cost per unit of commodities produced.

Another possible benefit of mechanisation and automation is improvement in quality, as more control and checks can be made.

In a sense, mechanisation could increase employment. Here I am referring to higher levels of manpower, e.g. technicians. As a result of this the levels of employment skills could be raised. Finally, new, small industries supplying components for the large mechanised businesses could be set up, thus increasing employment.

Having said all this, we must remember that mechanisation could produce a conflict with the present policy of promoting labour intensive industries. Indeed, conflict could arise from the trade unions which would be protecting the interest of workers, who could well find themselves out of work as mechanisation is introduced. Thus, mechanisation and automation are likely to increase unemployment of unskilled labour.

Questions

1 Define: (i) industry; (ii) cottage industry; (iii) linkage industry.
2 Make a list of cottage industries found in your country and say whether the raw materials used in each are local or imported.
3 Choose an industry and show how it could develop forward and backward linkages.
4 What effect would mechanisation and automation have on industries in your country?

6　Business organisation

Role and functions of a business

In this chapter we shall be looking at the different types of business organisations. However, before we can examine business units, we should answer the question: what are the functions of a business?

There are several reasons why an individual or individuals may go into a business enterprise. The main reason, however, is to make a profit. If there is no likelihood of making a profit then no-one would go into business. Having decided that there is the possibility of making a profit, then there are other considerations or objectives:

(a)　to provide a service to the community;
(b)　to provide employment;
(c)　to promote the well-being of employees;
(d)　to promote local industry;
(e)　to increase yearly sales;
(f)　to secure prestige;
(g)　the satisfaction of being one's own boss.

Each business provides some service, tangible or intangible, to the community; e.g. a bakery provides bread, a bank provides banking services. Most businesses provide employment for people in the community; this is a major function of a business. Moreover, if the business is to be run efficiently, then the welfare of the employees must be considered. In this respect some businesses lead to the development of skills of workers, and also provide them with opportunities for further education.

The promotion of local industry, using local raw materials, can be an important function of some industries, e.g. handicraft in the Caribbean. Finally, an important objective of the owner is consumer satisfaction and increased yearly sales to maintain the profitability of the business.

The need for capital (finance)

In order to start a business, no matter how small, finance is needed. The owner of a business needs finance (i) to purchase assets, for example factory, machines (fixed capital) and (ii) to meet day-to-day expenses (working capital). Having started the business, finance is needed for further expansion, to meet overhead expenses, to purchase and maintain a well balanced stock and to meet operational and maintenance costs.

There are generally four main sources of capital: (i) personal savings; (ii) borrowing from commercial banks or some other financial institution; (iii) raising capital on the market by issuing shares to the public; (iv) ploughed back profits.

Business units

Broadly speaking there are two main groups of business units:
(a) *Private enterprise*
   (i) Sole trader
   (ii) Partnerships
   (iii) Joint stock companies: private, public
   (iv) Cooperative societies
(b) *Public enterprise*
   (i) Public corporations
   (ii) Municipal undertakings

SOLE TRADER
The sole trader is a person who is in business on his own in the sense that he himself bears the entire risk of his own business operations and that he takes any profit which the business may yield. He may be employing others to work in his business, but these persons would be employed at a wage and their employment would not affect the risk which he takes personally.

Advantages
(a) Business is simple to start as it generally requires only a small amount of capital and no legal formalities.
(b) Decisions can be made promptly and new ideas can be put into operation quickly.
(c) There is close personal contact with employees and customers which makes for good personal relations with employees and an understanding of customers' needs.

(d) There is personal incentive to succeed and to run the business efficiently.

(e) Organisation can be flexible.

Disadvantages

(a) The sole trader must find all the capital needed to start the business and for later expansion. This limits the size of the business.

(b) The sole trader has to work long hours and may not be able to take a vacation.

(c) When he dies the business may have to be closed down as there may be no-one to continue the business.

(d) The sole trader has unlimited liability which means he may lose not only the money invested in the business, but even his personal property and savings if the business fails.

PARTNERSHIPS

An ordinary partnership is an association of between two and twenty persons who are in business in common with a view to earning a profit. In the case of a limited partnership, there must be at least one general partner (a member of the firm who is willing to accept responsibility for all debts incurred by the business). The other partners (limited partners) only contribute capital to the firm. Limited partnerships are not very common because private companies are just as easy to form.

It is good business practice to draw up a deed or agreement of partnership which must be signed by the partners. The deed must embody all important terms or features of the partnership. In the event of a dispute between the partners, the deed would be produced as evidence in a court of law. In the absence of an agreement as to how profits are to be shared, profits and losses would be shared equally.

Advantages

(a) As with a sole trader, a partnership is easy to form without legal formalities.

(b) More capital can be raised by the combined resources of a number of partners.

(c) Specialisation in management is possible as each partner may participate in the field in which he has experience and training.

(d) In a partnership the work load can be shared among the partners. This makes it possible for a partner to take a vacation and, on the death of a partner, the remaining partners can continue to run the business on their own, or they may find a new partner.

(e) There is still the incentive to succeed and there is also close contact with employees and customers.

Disadvantages
(a) All the partners stand to lose if one partner makes a bad mistake.
(b) Capital is still limited.
(c) Except in the case of a limited partnership, there is still unlimited liability if the business fails.
(d) There is the risk of disagreement and quarrelling with other members of the firm.

JOINT STOCK COMPANIES

A joint stock company is an association of persons who have contributed capital towards the operating of a business. A joint stock company is a legal person; it has an existence separate from that of the persons who own it: the shareholders. The owners contribute capital towards the company by buying shares in it and they enjoy the benefits of limited liability which means that in the event of the company failing, they may lose the fully paid-up value of the shares and nothing else. There are two classes of joint stock companies: public companies and private companies.

Private companies
(a) No shares or debentures can be offered to the general public.
(b) Shares are not transferable without the consent of the company's directors.
(c) The company's accounts are private.
(d) The number of members will not be less than two or more than fifty, not counting employee shareholders.

Public companies
(a) Shares and debentures are advertised and offered to the general public.
(b) Shares are easily transferable, via a stock exchange if one exists or through Trust Companies.
(c) All accounts must be made public and must be submitted to the Registrar of Companies.
(d) The number of members must not be less than seven.

Formation of a joint stock company
Essential information must be forwarded to the Registrar of Companies, for example, name of company, objectives, method of finance. Each company must submit
(a) a Memorandum of Association or Charter, spelling out the name, objectives, country of operations, capital authorised, and a declaration of limited liability.
(b) Articles of Association which spell out:
    (i) the rights and priorities of members at meetings;

(ii) the division of shares into classes with strict identification of shareholders' rights and priorities;
(iii) share transfer and forfeiture procedure;
(iv) borrowing powers of the company;
(v) the procedure for re-election of directors;
(vi) the powers of the directors;
(vii) the procedure for the calling up of uncalled capital.

The Memorandum of Association governs the external relationships (outside) of the company, while the Articles of Association govern the internal relationships.

The Prospectus of the company contains information about new shares to be issued and invites the public to make offers to buy on the terms and conditions set out in the prospectus.

After the memorandum and articles have been filed with the registrar, accompanied by a list of people consenting to act as directors and a statutory declaration to this effect, the registrar will issue a Certificate of Incorporation.

Shares

The holders of shares are part-owners of the business and will share in the company's profits by receiving dividends.

1 **Ordinary shares** Holders of these are the real risk-bearers of the company. It is these people who will get no returns if the company is doing badly.
2 **Preference shares** These are offered at a fixed rate of dividend. Preference shareholders must be paid their fixed rate of dividend before ordinary shareholders can receive dividends. However, if the company makes no profit then the holders will not receive any dividend for that year.
3 **Cumulative preference shares** The holders of these will have to be paid arrears of dividends by the company at some future date before dividends are paid to the other shareholders, if the company returns to profitability.
4 **Founders shares** These are issued to the founders or promoters of the company for their services in formation and are at the bottom of the priority list.

Debentures

Debentures are loan certificates offered at multiples of a basic figure, e.g. $100, and they carry interest at a fixed rate. This interest must be paid whether or not a profit has been made.

Advantages of limited liability companies

(a) Large sums of money can be raised by issuing shares.
(b) Shares are easily transferable through a security exchange or through

other agencies.

(c) Limited liability is a great boon to investors.

(d) There is continuity of existence.

(e) The company is a separate subject for taxation.

(f) It provides an outlet for savings, in the form of investment. (The public issue of shares mobilises the savings of many people whose money would not otherwise find its way into productive uses.)

(g) Specialisation and research are encouraged.

(h) Economies of scale are possible. Economies of scale are the benefits to be derived from large-scale production.

Disadvantages of limited liability companies

(a) Management is divorced from ownership.

(b) There is little contact between owners and employees or customers.

(c) A company cannot be formed easily.

(d) There can be reduced incentives to work hard since managers are not owners.

COOPERATIVE SOCIETIES

A cooperative is a business organisation that is owned and operated by its members. Members are generally a group of people with corresponding interests who have established the cooperative society for their mutual benefit. Membership is gained by buying shares, as in any other business. The shares usually have a low value, such as $1, $5, or $10. The number of shares which a member may hold is limited, but irrespective of the number of shares held, a member may cast one vote only at general meetings of the society.

The members of the society elect a board of management which will operate the business on behalf of its members.

The main purpose of a cooperative is to serve its members, and any profits derived from the fulfilment of this purpose are distributed among members.

Consumer cooperatives

The consumer cooperative society is common in many Caribbean territories, and takes many forms, from a simple 'Buying Club' to cooperative supermarkets. The purpose is the joint purchase of commodities by two or more persons. By making a joint purchase a large quantity may be purchased at a lower price. This results in a saving for each individual. In a larger cooperative, business members receive a rebate from profits in proportion to their purchases. This is usually referred to as patronage dividends.

In some cases retail cooperatives get together and organise a wholesale cooperative to supply members with commodities.

Farmers' cooperatives

These are common in the Windward Islands especially among small banana growers. They assist the farmers in such areas as production, marketing and purchasing. For example, fertiliser is purchased in bulk and sold at a low price to members, and, in many cases, the crop is marketed by the cooperative. Such farmers' cooperatives relieve the farmer of many of the details of selling and supply his needs for fertiliser, seeds, sprays and boxes.

Some producers' cooperatives have been organised to produce chicken hatcheries, creameries, etc.

Advantages

(a) There is a guaranteed market for members.
(b) Little or no advertising costs are incurred.
(c) There is no profiteering.
(d) There is democratic form of management.
(e) Economies of bulk buying are available to all members.
(f) Employment is created within the organisation.
(g) They can be useful as government agencies.

Disadvantages

(a) Management may be poor and inexperienced.
(b) Conflict may arise when members are both employers and employees.
(c) Lack of capital may cause problems.

Trade associations and chambers of commerce

In the Caribbean, a number of representative and regulatory bodies whose functions are to promote the interests of trade, commerce and manufacturers have been established in several of the Caricom markets in both the private sector and the public sector. Trade associations differ from chambers of commerce in that, while chambers of commerce usually represent businesses of all kinds, trade associations represent the interests of one particular group.

THE PRIVATE SECTOR

Chambers of commerce are the oldest promotional and regulatory bodies of their kind in the common market, and were founded by the private sector in the nineteenth century. They act as representatives of the commercial sectors in dealing with government on issues which affect their members. Their main functions are:

(a) to promote measures calculated to benefit and protect the trading interests of their members and trade in general;

37

(b) to undertake by arbitration or otherwise the settlement of disputes arising out of trade, commerce or industry;
(c) to promote and encourage the development of manufacturing operations, suitable to the community in which they exist, and capable of making contributions to the economic welfare and development of the country;
(d) to encourage and assist manufacturers in the use of efficient and modern methods of manufacture and maintenance and proper standards of safety, labour relations, employees' welfare, public relations and advertising;
(e) to promote and encourage adherence by manufacturers to proper standards and grades of quality in all manufactured products;
(f) to assist in securing markets for both raw materials and finished products;
(g) to discuss together problems affecting local (or regional) manufacturing industries and to take such action as they think fit;
(h) to collect and disseminate statistical or other information relating to trade and industry, imports and exports, manufacturing processes and developments, wages and labour conditions, and any other matters that may be in their interest;
(i) to promote, support or lawfully oppose any measures affecting the interest of the chambers.

Manufacturers' associations

With the advent of manufacturing industries in the region, several countries have Manufacturer's Associations. The main functions of these organisations are:
(a) to liaise with government in promoting the development of trade and industry;
(b) to provide a recognised central forum for consultation on and discussion of matters affecting manufacturers;
(c) to assist in securing markets for finished products;
(d) to assist in the development of proper trading standards and encourage adherence to same;
(e) to collect and disseminate statistical and other relevant information relating to trade and industry, imports and exports, manufacturing processes and development, and other matters of interest to manufacturers;
(f) to encourage and assist manufacturers in the use of efficient and modern methods of manufacture, and the maintenance of proper standards of safety, labour relations, wages, employees' welfare,

public relations and advertising;

(g) to promote and encourage the use by consumers of local manufacturers in their market.

Small business associations

Another new organisation in the region is the Small Businesses Association, branches of which are found in a few of the islands. The functions of this organisation are:

(a) to promote good relations between small businesses;
(b) to assist in the development of small businesses;
(c) to create public awareness of the small business sector and its importance in the national economy;
(d) to demonstrate the quality and variety of local products and services of the small business sector and thereby promote consumer acceptance and support;
(e) to operate as a pressure group to get assistance from government, commercial banks, etc. for small businesses.

Employers' associations

These associations have as their main function the regulation of relations between employees and employers, and the promotion of the interests of employers, in particular:

(a) to collect, collate and circulate information for the guidance of members, and to keep them informed on national and international movements in industrial relations and where necessary to represent them with regard to the operations of existing laws, legislative proposals and the activities of government which may affect the interest of employers;
(b) to encourage by negotiation and by arbitration the settlement of differences and disputes between employees and any of the members or groups of members of the association;
(c) to face union pressure for wage increases. An Employers' Association is far better equipped to do so than are individual employers.

Questions

1   The main objective of a business is to maximise profits. How true is this statement?
2   Mr Jones started a business as a sole trader, after many years his business becomes a public joint stock company. Show the possible

stages Mr Jones' business might have gone through and give the advantages and disadvantages of each stage.

3   Why do companies need finance?
4   List the types of shares which a company might issue.
5   Distinguish between a trade association and a chamber of commerce.

7 Organisation of production

Having examined business organisations in the previous chapter, we now turn our attention to the organisation of production. In this chapter we shall look at three of the major decisions which an entrepreneur has to make once the type of business organisation has been decided upon. These are (i) the location of his enterprise; (ii) the size; (iii) the proportions in which he employs the factors of production.

Location of industry

The major factor affecting the location of a factory is cost, i.e. how much in actual dollars and cents it would cost to locate the factory at the given site, and how the site chosen would affect future running expenses.

In every type of production, the entrepreneur requires raw materials of various kinds, fuel and labour, and he will have to transport the finished product to its market or markets. If we leave aside the question of labour supply for the moment, we find that both raw materials and fuel can be transported, but at a cost. If the site chosen is near the sources of raw materials and a supply of fuel, the cost of transporting these may be low. If the site is far from the market, the cost of carrying the finished product there will be high. If the site selected is near the market but far from the sources of materials and fuel, then the cost of transporting the finished product will be low.

In considering the site for his enterprise, the entrepreneur, whether local or foreign, must consider several factors.

1 **Raw Materials** Are they available locally or would they have to be imported? If imported, is it from within the region or outside?
2 **Market** Is the enterprise for the local market only, or is it for the regional market, or is it for local, regional and world? The size of and accessibility to the market or markets is very important.
3 **Land** Is the site suitable for producing the given commodity? Is

41

land available for future expansion or for erecting recreational facilities for workers? Is sufficient space available on government industrial estates?

4   **Labour** Is there an adequate supply of local labour? Can local labour be easily trained? What are the wage rates locally, and what type of union/management relationship exists? Can workers get to work easily?

5   **Infrastructural services (power, water, transportation, etc.)** Are there adequate supplies of water, lighting, sources of power, air and seaport facilities, a good road network and transportation facilities? How good are the communication services, e.g. telephone, telegraph, telex, etc.? Is the postal service reliable?

6   **Political stability** How stable, politically, is the country?

Economies of scale

As a firm or industry expands, it is able to secure certain benefits that are not available to small firms or industry. These benefits are called economies of scale. Economies of scale can be either internal, relating mainly to the firm or plant, or external, relating to the industry. The benefits or internal economies which large firms enjoy over small firms are of five main types:

(a)   technical savings;
(b)   reduced financial risk;
(c)   lower cost of finance;
(d)   lower purchasing costs;
(e)   specialisation in management.

TECHNICAL SAVINGS
These originate from the size of the firm itself. A small printer could never find enough work to warrant the purchase of a large offset litho type machine, whereas, in a large printing firm, the use of these machines can be justified. Not only would it cut down on the number of staff required, but the fixed cost could be spread over a larger number of units. Technical savings also arise from being able to make processes continuous: a motor car assembly plant with twice the capacity of a smaller one does not cost twice as much to operate.

REDUCED FINANCIAL RISK
Large firms which mass-produce in large quantities usually sell in many markets. This helps to avoid fluctuations in the volume of output that could raise costs. Large firms also make different commodities in order

to reduce the risk of loss and of fluctuations in production, owing to changes in people's tastes. Large firms also try to reduce the costs which could result if one source of raw materials dries up by purchasing raw materials from different sources.

LOWER COST OF FINANCE
As firms grow they acquire 'Good will'. They become 'household names' which are well known to the public and they generally acquire massive financial resources. Thus, they find it easier to borrow from banks who might actually compete for their account. They can also borrow at a lower cost than small firms. Good will and a reputation for sound financial management also make it easier for them to borrow by issuing debentures or preference shares. Large firms can use traders' credit accounts, paying one bulk cheque to their own bank rather than several cheques. Thus they reduce their bank and cheque charges and economise on payments to suppliers.

LOWER PURCHASING COSTS
Large firms buy in large quantities thus gaining a 'monopoly-buyer' advantage bringing down the price to the lowest possible figure.

SPECIALISATION IN MANAGEMENT
Large firms economise on managerial skill which is a scarce commodity. A manager and his assistant can probably control a plant employing 1,000 workers. If there were five plants, each with a manager and an assistant, but with a combined work force of 1,000, then the managers of those individual plants would be under-utilised, and the total salary for the five managers and assistants would be several times higher than that of one manager and an assistant. At the top level, directors can specialise in sales, accounting, production and research, thus bringing the directors into direct contact with what is going on in the firm and eliminating 'red tape' and loss of time. There can be specialisation of managers in a large firm.

ROLE AND FUNCTIONS OF SMALL FIRMS
While it is definite that large firms have clear advantages over small firms, there is still a place for small firms in the economy. In fact small firms tend to predominate in the Caribbean. There are several reasons why this is so.
(a) The small firm of today is the large firm of tomorrow. The growth of future business depends upon the growth of small business.
(b) Small businesses provide services not provided by big businesses.

(c) The degree of precision needed may preclude too much mechanisation.

(d) The product may be wholly a personal service.

INTERNAL DISECONOMIES

As the firm begins to expand, it places a strain on such indivisible factors as managerial ability. These strains result in certain drawbacks which are referred to as diseconomies of scale. As the firm continues to increase, the indivisible factors must be duplicated and thus will not only increase average costs, but also cause difficulties to management in coordinating the work of the factors used in the process of production. A firm may expand up to a point and enjoy the advantages of increasing returns (see below), but if it were to get any bigger, diminishing returns would set in. When the firm has reached an ideal size it should cease to expand, because at this point it is at its optimum.

EXTERNAL ECONOMIES

A firm may enjoy certain advantages not through its own expansion, but by being in a well organised and large industry. The benefits resulting from being part of a well organised and large industry are called external economies of scale.

A well organised industry enjoys certain research facilities which are available to all firms in the industry. Education and training facilities are available as well in such an industry, and firms find it easy to secure the right kind of training for their staff.

Industries which are well organised generally have very good marketing arrangements through which they can purchase raw materials and sell their final products. There are also facilities for representing the entire industry in foreign markets, and for collective advertising of the industry's goods. In the Caribbean, the tourist industry is a very good example. Also, in such industries, common services are available to be drawn upon by firms. Examples are special transport facilities or special treatment from bankers who have become acquainted with the particular needs of the industry.

EXTERNAL DISECONOMIES

We saw that certain diseconomies limit the amount of expansion which a firm may undertake. There are also certain diseconomies associated with the industry. These are external diseconomies.

As industry grows, there will be an increasing demand for raw materials mainly used in the industry. This will have the effect of forcing up the prices of those materials, and as a consequence, the firm's costs.

The same will apply also to the skilled labour which is mainly employed in the industry. Wage rates will be forced up as firms compete for the services of the skilled workers available. Moreover, as the number of firms increases and competition becomes stiffer, more will have to be spent on advertising if the firm is to maintain its position. Prices will have to be cut as far as possible to be able to sell at all.

The Law of Variable Returns

The entrepreneur combines the various factors of production with a view to obtaining the highest possible returns. To achieve this, he must study carefully the relationship between the quantities of factors which he uses (input) and the quantities of product which he obtains (output). Assume that a farmer is combining two factors, (i) land, which is fixed in quantity and (ii) labour, which varies. The farmer will discover by a process of trial and error the situation illustrated below.

No. of labourers	Total output	Output per labourer	Marginal outputs
1	20	20	20
2	60	30	40
3	114	38	54
4	156	39	42
5	170	34	14
6	174	29	4

The Law of Variable Returns states that when increasing quantities of one or more variable factors are used in combination with a fixed factor, there will come a point when first the marginal product (i.e. the increase in output resulting from introduction of an additional unit of the variable factor), and then the average product (i.e. output per labourer), will diminish.

The point where average product is at its highest is the optimum combination of factors. In our example the optimum combination is four units of labour.

The Law of Variable Returns consists of two parts: the law of increasing returns and the law of diminishing returns. Up to the optimum point average returns are rising because we are dealing with a fixed factor which is indivisible, and which, unless used to its fullest extent, is under-employed. After the optimum point is reached and passed, average returns will fall.

The reason for this stage is that factors of production are not perfect substitutes for each other. If labour could be substituted for land then all over-populated countries would be able to produce all the food which is required from one single acre of land.

The Law of Variable Returns is a physical law concerned solely with the process of production and does not as such tell us anything about the actual level of production which it would be desirable to aim for. Secondly, the law is true at any one time, but it would not be proper to compare the position between two separate points of time. Thirdly, we are assuming that the units of variable factors which are added to the fixed factors are homogeneous, e.g. that each labourer is of equal efficiency. This is not necessarily true and diminishing returns may set in earlier if the additional worker were of a poorer quality than the previous one or ones. Fourthly, the law applies only where the proportion in which the factors can be combined is a variable one. In some cases, for technical reasons, the proportion may be fixed. In these cases, the law cannot be applied.

Questions

1 What factors would a businessman take into account when deciding upon the site for his factory?
2 Distinguish between internal and external economies of scale.
3 Examine critically the Law of Variable Returns.

8   Management

Functions and responsibilities

The term 'management' is one which is not easily defined, although textbooks generally attempt some form of loose definition. In this text we shall define management as a social process entailing responsibility for the effective and economic planning and regulation of the operations of an enterprise, in fulfilment of a given purpose, or task. Management, then, has the responsibility for planning, organising, operating and controlling a firm or organisation.

In this book when the term management is used, it refers not merely to top management, but to all levels of management, e.g. the departmental head and the foreman. Management includes all those people in the organisation from the top man to the line supervisor and all administrative levels in between.

In its widest sense the functions of management involve the following activities.

(a) Planning, which comprises the formulations of the overall policy of the business enterprise concerned. This is the responsibility of top management. Planning also involves the formulation of an organisation structure defining the duties and responsibilities of the personnel employed, and the manner in which their activities are to be interrelated. Finally, planning means outlining duties of 'functional' and 'line' managers who are the administrators.

(b) Forecasting of sales, production, costs, capital expenditure, cost requirement, etc. as a preliminary to planning.

(c) Control, an effective system of which is essential, to check achievements against the plans and to supply management at all levels with information concerning any deviations between plans and actual performance. Then, when necessary, corrective action may be taken promptly.

(d) Motivation is an essential part of management functions. Since success rests ultimately in the hands of the employees, management must lead and inspire those upon whom it relies to implement its policy and make the organisation work. Motivation is done through the following:

    (i) a pleasant working environment;
    (ii) the promise of job security;
    (iii) proper channels of communications;
    (iv) providing avenues for self-expression;
    (v) recognition of the ability of workers;
    (vi) proper leadership style;
    (vii) wages, the levels as well as the system of paying.

(e) Coordination of activities.

RESPONSIBILITIES OF MANAGEMENT

Here we shall consider the responsibilities of 'top management'.

1 **Fiduciary** The directors are trustees of the company's property and of the powers entrusted to them by the shareholders. They are agents for the company and have the power to bind it, acting within the scope of their authority. This is a legislative function.

2 **To earn maximum profits** Some regard this as the primary responsibility of management to the shareholders who are the actual owners of the enterprise. Management must strive to maximise profits so that the shareholders can be sure of a reasonable return on their investment. They must also provide shareholders with up-to-date information concerning the company's present activities and the board proposals for future development.

3 **Formulation of policy** It is the responsibility of management to determine and state the company's policy in line with the Companies Acts.

4 **Social responsibility**
    (i) To produce goods of high quality and service at a reasonable price, and to carry out fair trading practices.
    (ii) To increase productivity and improve the quality of goods supplied to the public, and to pass on savings to the consumer.
    (iii) To provide opportunity for training at all levels, and to provide incentives for promotion.
    (iv) To try to create good human relationships in industry.

Management, therefore, consists of activities undertaken by one or more persons to coordinate the activities of other persons to achieve results not achievable by one person acting alone. The manager must achieve results through (i) coordinated work, (ii) planned, organised and controlled work, and (iii) work-related and person-related activities.

48

PRINCIPLES OF MANAGEMENT

The problem as to what constitutes sound management has been the subject of much study and debate by writers on management. The principles outlined below are considered to be a very important aspect of any organisation.

PRINCIPLES OF SOUND ORGANISATION

1 **Unity of direction** Each group of organisational activities that have the same objective should be directed by one manager using one plan.

2 **The scalar chain** The line of authority from top management to the lowest ranks represents the scalar chain. All communications should follow this chain, but if following the chain creates delays, cross-communications can be allowed if agreed to by all parties and if superiors are kept informed.

3 **Unity of command** Each person should answer to only one superior.

4 **Simplification, specialisation and standardisation** These concepts should be introduced and encouraged whenever possible in an organisation.

5 **Order** People and materials should be in the right place at the right time.

6 **Equity** Managers should be kind and fair to their subordinates.

7 **Discipline** Employees need to obey and respect the rules of the organisation. Good discipline is the result of effective leadership, a clear understanding between management and workers regarding the organisation's rules, and the judicious use of penalties for infractions of the rules.

8 **Subordination of individual interests to the general interest** The interests of any one employee or group of employees should not take precedence over the interests of the organisation as a whole.

9 **Remuneration** Workers must be paid a fair wage for their services.

10 **Authority** Managers need to be able to give orders. Authority gives them this right. Responsibility goes along with authority. Whenever authority is exercised, responsibility arises.

11 **Stability of tenure of personnel** High employee turnover is inefficient. Management should provide orderly personnel planning and ensure replacements are available to fill vacancies.

12 **Initiative** Employees who are allowed to originate and carry out plans will exert high levels of effort.

13 **Esprit de corps** Promoting team spirit will build harmony and unity within the organisation.

14 **Centralisation**   This is the degree to which subordinates are involved in decision-making. Whether decision-making is centralised (left to management) or decentralised (involving subordinates) is a question of the right proportion. The problem here is to find the right degree of centralisation for each situation.

15 **Motivation**   We have already seen that motivation is an important function of management. We shall now spend some time examining a few more aspects of motivation.

MOTIVATION
Motivation is the term given to the process of satisfying needs. It is concerned with the 'why' of human behaviour — what it is that makes people do things.

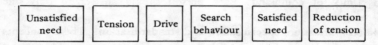

The process of motivation

The motivation of employees is a very important factor in the success of any business organisation. Managers must therefore be familiar with the theories of motivation. Here we shall look briefly at three of these theories.

The Hierarchy of Needs Theory
This theory was put forward by Abraham Manslow, who said that within every human being there exists a hierarchy of five needs. These are:
  (i) physiological needs — hunger, thirst, shelter, and other bodily needs;
 (ii) safety needs — these include security and protection from physical and emotional harm;
(iii) social needs — affection, acceptance, friendship, etc.;
(iv) esteem needs — including internal esteem factors such as self-respect, autonomy and achievement, and such external factors as status, recognition and attention;
 (v) self-actualisation needs — growth, achieving one's potential, and self-fulfilment, it is the drive to become what one is capable of becoming.

Theory X and Theory Y
Douglas McGregor proposed that managers have two distinct views of

human nature, one basically negative, which he calls Theory X, and another basically positive, which he calls Theory Y. Those managers holding the Theory X view assume that subordinates need to be coerced, controlled and threatened. Such actions are needed because employees

(a) inherently dislike work and whenever possible will attempt to avoid it;
(b) dislike responsibilities for decision-making;
(c) have little ambition and want job security above all.

On the other hand those managers holding the Theory Y point of view assume that employees are

(a) not lazy and want to do challenging work;
(b) interested, under proper conditions, in accepting responsibility;
(c) interested in displaying ingenuity and creativity.

Motivation-Hygiene Theory
Frederick Herzberg based his theory on research done on 200 engineers and accountants. According to Herzberg, some conditions operate chiefly to dissatisfy employees when the conditions are not present, but the presence of these conditions does not build *strong* motivation. He called these factors 'maintenance' or 'hygiene' factors since they are necessary to maintain a *reasonable* level of satisfaction. These factors are:

(a) company policy and administration;
(b) salary;
(c) job security;
(d) technical supervision;
(e) status;
(f) personal life;
(g) working conditions;
(h) inter-personal relations with superiors;
(i) inter-personal relations with subordinates.

Another set of conditions builds up *high* levels of motivation and job satisfaction. If these conditions are not present, they do not prove highly dissatisfying, however, to employees. These factors are 'motivational' factors or satisfiers:

(a) achievement;
(b) recognition;
(c) advancement;
(d) the work itself;
(e) the possibility of personal growth;
(f) responsibility.

These three theories are about the best known of all the theories on motivation. Note that in many respects they are similar.

LEADERSHIP OR MANAGEMENT STYLES

Leadership may be described as the process of influencing the activities of an organised group in an effort to provide goal-setting and goal-achievement. In business, leadership involves combining personal leadership abilities with good management techniques. Generally speaking there are three major leadership styles: autocratic, employee-centred and democratic.

Autocratic leadership is based on the old authoritarian school of management which holds the view that management should do the thinking, give the orders and closely control activities through personal supervision. Authority is here closely associated with power. Management sees its authority as the right to manage, to command and act, coupled with ability to supply or withhold what people want, to hire and fire, to promote or not to promote, to control wages, output, etc. Authoritarian administration is also associated with capitalisation of planning and control, and with the situation where the administrator is either reluctant or unable to delegate responsibility to others. Such management style stifles initiative and innovation at the middle management level. Employees are little motivated to do their job well under authoritarian leadership.

Employee-centred leadership is based on the concept that the leader is the representative of the group and carries out what the group wants done. He fulfils the wishes of the group and exerts what initiative the group desires him to have. Whenever management is small, e.g. a small firm with few directors, the employee-centred style of leadership may be both appropriate and effective. A small group working closely together needs little formal leadership, only occasional guidance. In such situations the chairman may function as a good reflector of the group's thinking and be able to carry out what the group wants done.

Democratic leadership is more of a middle ground. The leader takes initiative on his own, but he is also receptive to the group he leads but does not dominate. He ensures that everybody in the group receives fair treatment and is encouraged to take part, yet he remains capable of making decisions. This type of leadership gives the leader the necessary authority to control, while at the same time providing an open democratic atmosphere in which others may express their views and vote according to their convictions.

Above we have discussed three basic management styles. However, between the autocratic leadership style and employee-centred style there is a continuum of styles. The following diagram on page 53 illustrates this.

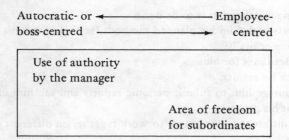

Autocratic- or ◄——————— Employee-
boss-centred ——————► centred

Use of authority
by the manager

Area of freedom
for subordinates

QUALITIES

The qualities needed to be a good manager are:

(a) knowledge or 'know how' of the enterprise and of business in general;
(b) dedication, and the ability to work hard and long hours;
(c) efficiency: the good manager must be efficient;
(d) the ability to get the cooperation of subordinates and employees;
(e) a good sense of humour;
(f) good leadership qualities;
(g) unquestionable integrity;
(h) tact;
(i) the ability to select the right persons for the right jobs;
(j) the ability to work with people, and to influence people to get tasks performed.

DELEGATION

Delegation may be defined as giving to others the responsibility for the performance of a specific task and for making decisions in a general or specific area of management activity. Delegation is the only way an administrator can spread his administrative talent and facilitate the necessary activities of his organisation. This is not easy to do, especially for managers with little training. For delegation to be effective, a manager must exercise control over a subordinate to whom he has delegated responsibility, but too much control destroys the very purpose of delegation. Delegation creates two responsibilities: the obligation to the leader of the person to whom authority is delegated, and that of the leader to those he represents. Since the leader who delegates authority retains accountability, he must maintain some form of supervision over his subordinates.

There are several ways to maintain control over a subordinate to whom authority has been delegated.

(a) Define clearly what is to be done.
(b) Discuss with him his planned method. He should submit a plan in writing or orally.
(c) Set deadlines for him.
(d) Check his results.
(e) Encourage him to submit periodic reports and ask him informally about his progress.
(f) Ask different subordinates to work together on different phases of plans.

Job design

The term job design refers to the way that tasks are combined to form a complete job. For example some jobs have tasks that are standardised and repetitive, others require a large number of varied and diverse skills, while yet others are narrow in scope. Today there are a number of alternative methods of job design which are designed for increasing employee satisfaction and productivity. We refer to these alternative methods as (QWL) quality of work-life programmes.

Job design programmes can be either individual programmes — programmes for designing or redesigning the tasks of individuals — or group programmes — designing jobs so as to increase the satisfaction and productivity of groups. Here we shall consider a few of these programmes.

First of all there is job rotation, which can be either vertical or lateral. Job rotation allows workers to diversify their activity and offset the occurrence of boredom. Vertical rotation relates to promotion and demotion. Lateral rotation allows employees to spend a few months on one activity and then move on to another. Job rotation broadens employees and gives them a wide range of experiences. Boredom and monopoly are reduced and employees are prepared more quickly to assume greater responsibility.

Work modules are another kind of programme and involve time task units equal to approximately two hours for a given task. A normal task of forty hours a week would then be defined in terms of four modules a day, five days a week for between forty-eight and fifty weeks a year. The benefits are that employees are allowed to pick their work tasks taking into account individual preferences. This system provides a way for boring and undesirable tasks to be completed without totally demoralising those people who must do them. Furthermore, jobs are constructed to meet the needs of the individual, rather than forcing him/her to fit into a particular, defined job.

The programme of job enlargement expands jobs horizontally. It increases the scope of a job: increasing the number of different operations required in a job and the frequency with which the job cycle is represented. For example if we take a post office sorter whose job is mainly to sort incoming mail, job enlargement would increase the scope of his job to include not only sorting, but also delivering mail to certain departments.

Job enrichment (even more effective than job enlargement) expands jobs vertically — it increases job depth. Job enrichment allows the employee greater control over his work. It allows him/her to assume some of the tasks typically done by his supervisor, for example planning, executing and evaluating the job. It allows an employee to do a complete job (activity) with increased freedom, independence and responsibility and provides feedback so that individuals can assess and correct their own performance.

The system of integrated work teams is job enlargement practised at the group level. The aim is to increase diversity for team members whose jobs require team-work and cooperation. In practice a team is assigned a large number of tasks. The group then decides the specific assignments of members and is responsible for rotating jobs among the members as the tasks require. There is a supervisor, who oversees the group's activities.

The system of autonomous work teams is job enrichment at the group level. The work which the team does is deepened through vertical integration. The team is given a goal to achieve and then is free to determine work assignments, rest breaks, inspection procedures, etc. The team may even select its own members and have the members evaluate one another's performance. Quality circle is a team of eight or ten employees and supervisors who have a shared area of responsibility. They meet regularly to discuss their quality problems, investigate causes and recommend solutions and then to take corrective action.

Flexitime is a scheduling system whereby employees are required to work a number of hours a week, but are free to vary their hours of work within certain limits.

The job characteristics model allows managers to analyse and identify five key job-characteristics called the Core Dimensions. These are:
(i) skill variety: the degree to which a job requires a variety of different activities so the worker can use a number of different skills and talents;
(ii) task identity: the degree to which the job requires completion of a whole or identifiable piece of work;
(iii) task significance: the degree to which the job has a substantial impact on the lives or work of other people;

(iv) autonomy: the degree to which the job provides substantial freedom, independence and discretion to the individual in scheduling the work and determining the procedures to be used in carrying it out;

(v) feedback: the degree to which carrying out the work activities required by the job results in the individual obtaining direct and clear information about the effectiveness of his/her performance.

CHANNELS OF INTERNAL COMMUNICATIONS

Communications is a very vital tool of management, and may be defined as the act (natural or artificial) of conveying information or giving instruction. All means of communication between employer and employee and between a company and its shareholders are important for several reasons.

(a) Employer-employee understanding is developed.

(b) Instruction and intelligence is communicated and imparted.

(c) The furthering of employees' interests.

(d) The shock of technological change is lessened.

(e) Future capital is more readily obtained.

(f) Employees are given opportunities for communication, back to their employers.

Broadly speaking, there are three major methods of communications: oral, written and visual.

Oral communications include joint consultation, meetings and conferences, interviewing, courses for trainees, speeches, personnel department, etc.

Written communications include agendas, annual reports, bulletins, correspondence, memoranda, minutes, manuals, journals and publications, etc.

Visual communication includes organisation charts, notice boards, microfilms, films and film strips, posters, statistical graphs, closed-circuit television, etc.

MANAGEMENT-WORKER RELATIONSHIPS

In every kind of business activity, management and labour need each other. It is therefore essential that a good working relationship exists between management and workers. Such a relationship should be based on an understanding of each other's problems, needs and responsibilities. It should be an understanding based on mutal respect and trust which would develop a climate that would engender mutual confidence. For such an atmosphere to develop, management should be easily approachable at all times.

In this respect it is the duty of the personnel manager to foster, maintain and improve the human relationships between management and personnel. It is his duty to make sure that personnel understands the policies of management, and that management in turn understands the problems and needs of workers. The personnel manager is responsible for education and training, the health and safety of workers, the general welfare of workers, wage negotiations and employment.

Internal organisation of a business

After the external form of organisation has been selected (sole trader, partnership, joint stock company or cooperative) it is necessary to set up the internal organisation. Regardless of the external form of business there must be a well-rounded, compact, and workable form of internal organisation. This is so because, for any business, regardless of the form in which it is operated, it still has the same functions to perform, and these functions usually determine the basis for internal organisation.

When a business is very small it is often possible for the owner to supervise all its activities. As soon as it has even a small growth, it becomes necessary for different men to be placed in charge of various functions. For example, if the business is a small manufacturing enterprise, it need only reach a moderate size before the owner must devote himself to either selling or manufacturing and obtain an assistant to supervise the other function. As growth continues the owner will need an office manager to be responsible for accounting records, customers' accounts and general office work. As the business continues to increase in size the need for further divisions of functions and additional executives will become apparent.

ORGANISATION OF TYPICAL MANUFACTURING ENTERPRISE
Major functional areas:

1   **Production** The function of this department is to plan and regulate the operation of that part of the enterprise which is responsible for the actual transformation of raw materials into finished products.

2   **Finance** The financial or accounts department is responsible for:
    (i) producing the annual balance sheet, including the profit and loss account, for presentation to the shareholders and to be filed with the Registrar of Companies;
    (ii) advising management on the availability of capital for expan-

sion and plant building and offering advice on how funds may raised;

(iii) making all payments and issuing receipts;

(iv) maintaining a satisfactory cash-flow position.

3 **Marketing** This department is responsible for:

    (i) assessing market possibilities by market research and sales forecasting;

   (ii) advertising and sales promotion;

  (iii) distribution of products.

The purpose is to ensure that the maximum profitable volume of the goods produced will be sold.

4 **Personnel** The function of this department is concerned with the recruitment of labour, its efficiency and training, the contentment of workers and with various aspects of welfare and medical care. In cases where there is not a separate public relations department, it is also responsible for public relations (maintaining good relations with the public).

TYPES OF ORGANISATION

1 **Line (or direct) organisation** This is sometimes called 'military' type. Here the lines of authority and responsibility are direct. For example, each department has a head who is in complete charge within the confines of his operations and is responsible to the Managing Director.

2 **Functional organisation** In this type of organisation departments are set up to carry out the basic functions. A special department is set up for each of the functions and the head of that department is responsible merely for that one function; for example, accounts, production, personnel.

3 **Line and staff** In this type of organisation the operating departments are set up with a head in charge of each. In addition a staff of specialists representing the various functions of the business is set up in each department to advise and assist that department.

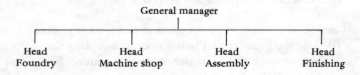

Line type of organisation

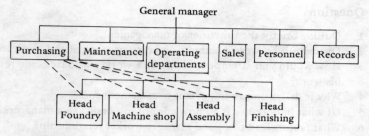

Functional type of organisation

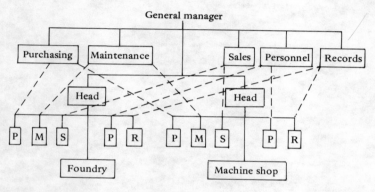

Typical line and staff organisation

4 **Committee type** This uses the principle of management specialisation in that a committee of specialists is assigned to advise the top executive and to assist him in developing policy and procedures.

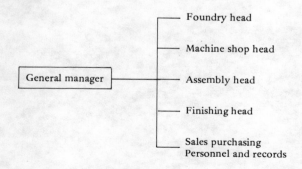

Committee organisation

Questions

1 Outline briefly the functions of management.
2 Distinguish between planning, forecasting, control and motivation.
3 How would you attempt to motivate a worker who lacks interest in his work?
4 Why is delegation an important management tool?
5 Of what importance is a knowledge of job design to a manager?
6 What factors lead to a good manager-worker relationship?
7 Distinguish between line, functional, and line and staff management organisations.

9   Labour

In the previous two chapters we discussed the decisions which an entrepreneur has to make and the functions and responsibilities of management. In this chapter we shall examine the decisions and problems of labour or the workers.

Why people work

Work may be defined as whatever people do in order to earn a livelihood. Man has always had to work to sustain himself, but work is more than just a biological necessity. It has also been a means of acquiring material possessions and power. In recent times two concepts of work have become prevalent. One is the notion that labour (work) was the origin of individual ownership and the source of all economic value. The other sees work as creative labour.

However, workers want more than just money. Once basic economic needs are satisfied (and even when they are not) workers are interested in job security. Apart from money and a secure job, workers want to feel that they are regarded and treated as human beings, that their human dignity is respected. They also want work that is challenging and an opportunity to exercise any talents they have or think they have. They want to have, or at least think they have, some share in the decision-making process in the work situation.

Unsatisfactory work experiences lead to job dissatisfaction or discontent, covert or overt, latent or expressed, to lack of interest and apparent laziness, to frustration and the brain-drain and sometimes to alienation, neuroses, and even more severe forms of mental illness.

Trade unions

A BRIEF HISTORY OF TRADE UNIONS DEVELOPMENT IN THE CARIBBEAN

In the Caribbean, when trade unions began they were virtually indistinguishable from labour movements. Both emerged as single anti-colonial mass movements with varying emphasis, at different stages and in different territories, on social, economic and politico-constitutional reforms. The young shoots of Caribbean trade unionism revealed themselves soon after World War I when a working class awakening and national consciousness emerged.

Before this a few workers' organisations existed which agitated on behalf of labour and some of which were truly trade unions, e.g. Trinidad Working Men's Association (late nineteenth century) organised by Alfred Richards. In Guyana attempts were made to organise workers into trade unions (Herbert Critchlow) and strikes were organised during the first decade of the twentieth century. In Jamaica, a number of pre-war craft unions existed, with which Marcus Garvey was associated. There was also a Tobacco Workers' Union and a local branch of the American Federation of Labour (The Jamaica Trades and Labour Union No. 16203).

The end of the war brought an upsurge in demand for the improvement of the working class conditions, accompanied by attempts to organise the working class and to create mass movements. In Jamaica a series of strikes took place between 1918 and 1919 in various industries and services.

At about this time (early twentieth century) in Jamaica, Bedwardism, a quasi-religious body of unemployed labourers, emerged. It was a camp of unemployed and discontents being indoctrinated with hostility to and total rejection of the society. However, more serious than Bedwardism was Garveyism. Its philosophy was one of negritude improvement and denunciation of the white-power regime. Garvey founded the People's Political Party in 1929 and this served as a lesson and proof of organisational possibilities of the working class. Both Bedwardism and Garveyism were mass movements alienated from the middle class.

In Trinidad the situation was different because, due to the composition of the population, leadership came from the middle class. Cipriani became President of the Trinidad Working Men's Association in 1919. His slogan was 'Agitate, Educate and Confederate'. He used this to condemn and oppose the existing colonial structure and to whip up national sentiment.

In Barbados the situation was one of resignation to the extreme rigid colour class structure. After World War I there was the development of a popular democratic movement (Clennel Wickham and C. Inniss); later the Democratic League was formed, (May 1924). This movement failed to bring about confrontation with the Establishment or to create any major social reform. Thus by the first quarter of the twentieth century, the struggle and role of the labour movement/trade unions was one of confrontation with the colonial powers and plantocracy-nationalism.

The next stage was during the 'period of disturbances' 1934-1939. The following chart shows how disturbed this period was:

May – July	1934	Disturbance on sugar estate in Trinidad
January	1935	Disturbance in St. Kitts
May	1935	Strike at Falmouth, Jamaica
Sept – Oct	1935	Disturbances in Guyana (then British Guiana)
October	1935	Riots in Kingstown and Camden Park
June	1937	General disturbances in Trinidad
July	1937	General disturbances in Barbados
May	1938	Disturbances in Frome, Jamaica
May – June	1938	General disturbances in Jamaica
February	1939	General disturbances in Guyana (then British Guiana)

The main cause of these disturbances was agitation for improved conditions for the masses and a less restricted way of life. In all territories society was pauperised and underdeveloped, conspicuously unjust with a rigid class stratification based on colour which led to job hierarchy.

This period saw the development of the true trade union organised labour movements. In Jamaica Norman Manley and Bustamante organised the B.I.I.U. which was later completely taken over by Bustamante. Manley then formed the N.W.U. The number of trade unions grew in all the islands and represented a wide variety of workers, a common feature being the alignment of trade unions with political parties.

Between 1939 and the present time the role of the trade unions as a base for mass support and the production of political leaders has continued, and has become one of the movement's main features throughout the Caribbean, except in Trinidad and Guyana where racial factors have now surpassed trade union ties. Besides this function, trade unions have been active in other areas. They have been responsible for generating a limited amount of mass solidarity. They have been able to secure political changes as well as social and economic benefits for the masses.

FUNCTIONS OF TRADE UNIONS

A trade union is an organisation of persons employed in an industry or following a particular trade who have joined together in order to improve their wages and working conditions. The main activities of trade unions are listed below.

1 **Collective bargaining**

A trade union which represents a substantial proportion of

employees in a firm (above fifty per cent) is in the position of a monopoly supplier of labour and has therefore greater bargaining power than the individual workers would have if they had to negotiate on their own for wages and working conditions.

The process of collective bargaining is fairly wide-spread and well established in the Caribbean. The system is modelled after the traditional British system and is self-administered, based upon the principle of freedom and voluntary negotiation. Labour and management are free to regulate their relationship, determine terms and conditions of employment and settle their problems by mutual consent.

There are two broad areas of collective bargaining in the Caribbean:

(i) bilateral determination of employment terms and conditions of work;

(ii) the application and administration of those terms and procedures agreed upon.

Collective bargaining is the process of negotiation of a contract between the representatives of labour and management. This process takes place on a voluntary basis without government interference. The negotiations may be opened by the presentation of proposals, usually by the representatives of labour. Generally these proposals are rejected by management's representatives and sometimes counter proposals are put forward by management. The give and take of bargaining then follows.

In the course of the negotiations each side has available the threat of economic force. On labour's side there are the weapons of go-slows, work-to-rule, sick-outs, and finally strike action with picketing. On management side there is the threat of lock-out or simply the refusal to accept labour demands.

In order for collective bargaining to take place smoothly, three conditions should be fulfilled:

(i)   It must be pursued with good sense on both sides. This comes from a tradition of good industrial relationships, and the establishment of some objective measure, e.g. cost of living index, the wage-rates paid in other trades or grades of work, or the profits being made by industry, to which wage-rates can be linked.

(ii)   Both sides must consist of strong organisations.

(iii) There must be an accepted procedure between the parties for dealing with questions as they arise. There are two stages of procedure: negotiations and settlement of disputes.

Negotiations

These can be:

(a) voluntary negotiations between the unions and employers' organisations,

(b) through joint industrial councils, e.g. Whitley Council;

(c) wages councils.

Settlement of disputes

In the Caribbean, labour legislation has been generally kept to the bare minimum, and usually takes the form of Minimum Wages Ordinances, Trade Disputes (Arbitration and Inquiry) Ordinance, and, in some cases, Public Utilities Undertaking and Essential Services Ordinances.

The machinery for the settlement of disputes generally proceeds in the following ways.

(a) The Chief Labour Officer (Commissioner) is instructed that a dispute exists. He then uses his office (conciliation) to try to get the parties to agree to a compromise solution.

(b) Some form of compulsory arbitration is decided upon. This means the settlement of the dispute by an outsider, or neutral person or persons. Such a person is called an arbitrator. Sometimes there may be a Board of Arbitrators or an Arbitration Court set up to handle the dispute.

(c) In cases where the Chief Labour Officer is not successful in getting the parties to come to some agreement, then the matter is brought to the notice of the Minister of Labour who may take any of several prescribed ways of settling the dispute. These include:

compulsory arbitration by a third person;

holding an inquiry into the dispute;

sending the dispute to an Industrial Court;

the minister himself trying to get the parties to reach an agreement.

(d) Industrial Courts, the decisions of which are binding on both parties, exist in some territories, e.g. Trinidad and Tobago (this country also has an Industrial Stabilisation Act), Antigua and Guyana.

2   **Social activities**

The union is the means through which employees may express their views not only on industrial matters but also on social issues. Some trade unions perform social functions by looking after the interests of their members who are sick, unemployed, recovering from illness or retired.

65

3   **Political activities**
     Trade unions have had, in the past, and still maintain even today, links with political parties. In many Caribbean islands the political leaders are also the trade union leaders in their countries. Some trade unions even sponsor members to run for political office.
4   **Educational activities**
     Many trade unions have set aside funds for the further education of their members and for children of members. There are also some trade union colleges in the region which offer courses in trade union principles and practices to their members.

TYPES OF UNIONS
1   **Craft Unions** These are unions in which all the members, irrespective of the industry in which they work, practise the same craft or trade and follow the same occupation, e.g. designers.
2   **Industrial Unions** As the name suggests, are unions in which all members are employed in the same industry, e.g. oil or bauxite.
3   **General Unions** These are very common in the Caribbean and are unions in which the members are of many trades and employed in many industries.
4   **Staff Unions** These are unions in which members are all white-collared workers (clerks and office staff).
     In many countries the trade unions have joined together to form congresses or councils, and in the Caribbean there is the Caribbean Congress of Labour with affiliate members in most West Indian Territories.

STRUCTURE OF TRADE UNIONS

General body
↓
Supreme policy-making body
↓
The Executive
provides effective leadership of the union
President
Vice President
Secretary, Assistant Secretary
Treasurer
Two or more committee members

↓
Shop stewards
located in plant in touch with
members and the committee

Simple structure

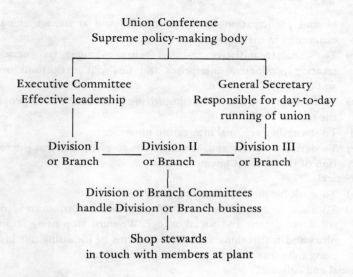

Union Conference
Supreme policy-making body

Executive Committee
Effective leadership

General Secretary
Responsible for day-to-day
running of union

Division I
or Branch

Division II
or Branch

Division III
or Branch

Division or Branch Committees
handle Division or Branch business

Shop stewards
in touch with members at plant

More complex union structure

EMPLOYERS' ASSOCIATIONS

In many countries wage negotiations are conducted by trade unions with employers' associations, e.g. in Barbados we have the Barbados Hotel Association and the Sugar Producer's Associations.

Employers are usually organised by industry and by area and these employers' associations serve as counterparts to the trade unions. There are also Caribbean Associations of employers, e.g. Caribbean Employers' Association.

Role of trade unions in a developing Caribbean

MAIN GOALS
(a) To achieve the economic and political emancipation of all W.I. people.
(b) To secure better wages and improved working conditions for the working classes.

FUTURE ROLE
To secure social justice and dignity for all classes.
Economic
(a) To foster greater economic independence and strengthening of economies by formulating policies aimed at more national control

of and participation in the economies and at strengthening the economies in the region.

(b) To stimulate initiative and self reliance among the masses by creating productive enterprises and financial institutions owned and controlled by unions.

(c) To find ways and means of improving know-how among people of the region.

(d) To strengthen regional integration movements.

(e) To devise strategies and contributions to plans aimed at the reduction of the levels of unemployment.

Political

(a) To work for political unity of the region.

(b) To assist in the development of an authentic Caribbean ideology for development and social change. We must stop using imported ideas and institutions and think in terms of localising our institutions and ideas.

Social and cultural

(a) To encourage an authentic W.I. culture.

(b) To assist in the organisation and greater expression of indigenous culture.

(c) To advise government about the restructuring of the educational systems in the region.

MOBILISATION OF LABOUR

The mobilisation of labour is essential if economic development is to become a reality in the region. Improvements in the quality of life for Caribbean peoples must come about through the development of self-reliance in all our communities; self-reliance of a kind which enables the region to make full use of all its resouces, especially its human resources. The question is how to mobilise labour in such a way that it will readily participate in communal self-help projects. Traditionally, most West Indian communities have practised some form of communal self-help project. For example, it was a common practice for relatives and friends to assist a neighbour in building his house. Also in most communities there are groups and organisations which carry out communal projects.

In some territories trained social workers and community developers play active roles in leading people into new activities within the villages. These social workers try to give people experience in organising themselves to solve problems by self-help and, just as important, to decide what they consider are their top-priority problems. The villagers are encouraged to decide what special developments they value most and to work for these developments by their own efforts rather than remaining passive objects of the national development programme. Through the assistance of these community developers, projects such as road building, laying drinking-water pipes, irrigation schemes and playgrounds for children have been undertaken in a number of villages.

More recent attempts at mobilisation of labour and the development of self-reliance has brought about the establishment of National Youth Services in many countries. In these schemes youths are required to do about two years of National Service. During those two years they participate in a number of national self-help projects such as road building, agriculture, etc. The idea of a Caribbean Volunteer Corps was put forward by the author of this book as far back as 1974. The C.V.C. was to function in a way similar to the American Peace Corps, but at the regional level. The idea was accepted by the Caricom Secretariat and an agreement was drawn up, but that was as far as it got.

Questions

1 Why, do you suppose, do people work?
2 Explain the process of collective bargaining and the settlement of disputes in the Caribbean.
3 What are the functions of a trade union?
4 What do you understand by the expression 'mobilisation of labour'? Why is it important?

10   Home trade

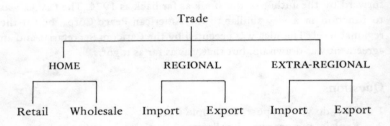

Aspects of trade

Trade may be defined as the exchange of commodities between producers or suppliers and customers at an agreed price.

Trade came into existence when men began to produce surplus goods as a result of specialisation. The earliest form of trade known to man is barter: the exchange of goods for goods. Modern trade has grown rapidly for the following reasons:

(a) the introduction of the factory system and division of labour;
(b) improvements in technology and the use of machinery;
(c) new inventions and new types of raw materials;
(d) new sources of power;
(e) increases in the working population;
(f) improvements in transportation;
(g) improvements in international trading relations.

Look at the diagram at the beginning of this chapter, and you will notice that trade in the Caribbean can be divided into three sections: home trade, regional (Caricom) trade, and extra-regional trade.

Home trade is the internal trade within each territory and takes place between buyers and sellers of commodities within a particular territory.

Home trade can be further subdivided into:

1   **Retail trade** This deals in small quantities and is the link between the wholesaler and the consumer;

2   **Wholesale trade** This deals in bulk purchases from the manufacturer and sells in small quantity to the retailer.

Regional trade means trade between the territories of the region, especially those who are members of the Caribbean Common Market Community. Such trade is governed by the Caricom Agreement.

Extra-regional trade is trade carried on between the territories in the region and countries outside the region. Foreign trade may be divided into:

1   **Import trade** This is the bringing of goods into the region or into a specific country or island;

2   **Export trade** This is the selling of goods to countries outside the island or to another territory.

Retail trade

The word retail comes from a French word meaning to 'cut up' and this is exactly what the retailer does. He purchases small quantities from the wholesaler and cuts this up into still smaller quantities to meet the needs of his customers. The retailer is the last link in the chain of production before the goods finally reach the consumer.

TYPES OF RETAILERS
There are two groups of retailers — small-scale retailers and large-scale retailers.

Small-scale retailers

Hawkers

These are common throughout the Caribbean. They sell a variety of goods including ground-provisions, vegetables, nuts and sweets. They usually sell from trays or in stalls located at a public market place or at street corners. Some travel around offering their goods for sale.

Itinerant pedlars

These are again common in the region. They travel from town to town or village to village selling mainly cloth, or garments, watches, etc. Formerly they travelled on foot carrying their goods in a suitcase (some still do today); motor cars are however becoming the standard means of transport today. Some of these itinerant pedlars offer customers a low rate of hire-purchase repayment.

Wayside drink sellers (mauby sellers)

These sell a variety of soft drinks, including mauby and ginger beer, cutters, e.g. fish cakes, salt-fish cutters, ham cutters, egg cutters, etc. to customers.

A hawker

Bar and groceries

Common throughout the Caribbean they sell mainly groceries, toiletries, pins, needles, etc. They also incorporate a section for the selling of liquor (bar). Some also sell cutters (and sandwiches) in the liquor section.

Apart from those mentioned above, there are other types of small retailers such as mobile shops, fruit vendors, vending machines, cook shops and small one-door or two-door stores.

Large-scale retailers

The main types of large-scale retailers found in the Caribbean are:

(a) trading companies;
(b) department stores;
(c) supermarkets;
(d) multiple shops and variety chain stores.

Trading companies

A trading company may be described as a number of business enterprises under one firm or ownership. A typical trading company may include hardware, lumber and building, home appliances, steamship agents and manufacturers' representatives.

All the operations may be carried out in one large complex or in different locations. There may be branches in different parts of the

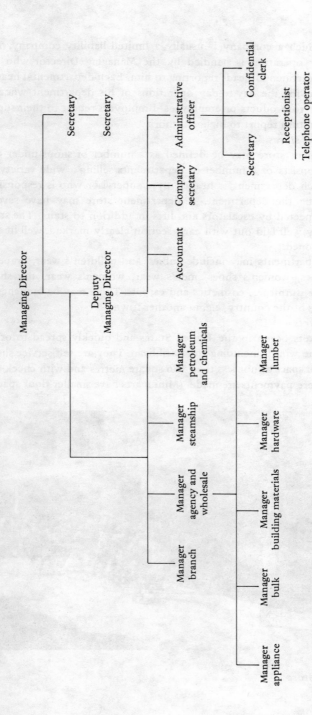

Structure of a typical trading company

country. Such a company is usually a limited liability company. The day-to-day operation is handled by the Managing Director who has several departmental heads reporting to him. Each departmental head is responsible for the day-to-day operations of his department whether they relate to products or employees. Employees report to their superiors who in turn report to higher authority.

Department stores

A department store may be defined as a number of shops under one roof. It consists of a number of departments selling a wide variety of goods. Each department is headed by a supervisor who is responsible for stocking the department. A department store may have several floors connected by escalators and lifts in addition to stairs. The store is generally well laid out with each section clearly marked, well lit and air conditioned.

The departments may include babies' and children's wear, drapery, men's shoes, women's shoes, men's wear, women's wear, toy shop, book store, furniture, cosmetics and carpets. There may be branches in other parts of the country, e.g. in another town.

Supermarkets

Supermarkets began in the United States and quickly spread to other parts of the world, including the Caribbean. They are self-service shops with a floor space of not less than 186 square metres and with check-out points where payments are made. (Mini marts have smaller floor space.)

A general store

They offer a wide range of foodstuffs, pre-packaged groceries, vegetables, meat and fish, fruit, drinks and liquors at prices lower than most of the small retailers. Supermarkets attract customers by offering specials and cut prices on certain goods (called loss leaders). The idea is that customers attracted to the supermarket by the loss leaders or specials would also purchase other goods (spontaneous shopping). Some supermarkets also offer Gold Bond stamps, samples, or run competitions to attract customers. Assistants are needed only for re-stocking shelves, general supervision, as a safeguard against pilfering, and as cashiers.

Multiple shops and variety chain stores

Multiple shops are small or medium-sized shops under one ownership. Originally the owner started with one shop which has multiplied into a number of single shops or branches sited at different locations within the territory.

Variety chain stores are larger multiple shops, being rather a combination of multiple shop and department store.

Multiple shops and variety chain stores are easily recognisable by the colour of their decoration, the style of window framework and the branded articles on sale. They offer a wide range of cheap general merchandise in a number of small departments spread over two or three floors. In the Caribbean the red and gold of Woolworth is well known in countries such as Barbados, Trinidad, Jamaica and formerly in Guyana. The big K of Kirpalani is also well known in a number of the

A typical shopping centre

islands, e.g. Trinidad, Barbados and Grenada.

Shopping plazas or arcades are now a common feature in many Caribbean islands. These offer a number of shopping and business facilities in one location. They are usually located just outside the city in an area offering parking facilities to customers. The shops sometimes stay open until late in the evening to accommodate customers coming from work. A typical shopping plaza may contain a supermarket, a hardware store, branches of department stores, a restaurant, a branch of a bank, a doctor's office and pharmacy. Thus customers are offered a wide range of facilities in one location.

Mail order selling

Mail order selling simply means 'shopping by post'. Some manufacturers, wholesalers and big retail organisations advertise their commodites through illustrated magazines, catalogues and newspapers sent to the public by post. The shop-window for the mail order firm is its catalogue which presents the customer with a wide range of goods attractively displayed. Housewives are appointed as agents for certain areas and accept responsibility for the collection of accounts from neighbours whom they have introduced to the scheme. The agents usually deduct a small percentage from each customer's repayments, then send the balance to the head office.

There are several advantages of mail order selling.

(a) Unlike shop windows, catalogues only need rearranging once a year and they do not need dusting.
(b) They make full use of the business reply service of the Post Office.
(c) They offer credit to customers and a money-back guarantee on any goods purchased.
(d) They offer a wide variety of goods to customers.
(e) Housewives are saved long journeys into town.
(f) They can undersell both retail shops and supermarkets because they have low overheads.

There are also several disadvantages.

(a) Catalogues are expensive to produce.
(b) The possibility exists of many bad debts building up.
(c) Customers cannot see the goods before they buy them.
(d) Agents might be dishonest.

The wholesale trade

Wholesalers are businessmen who handle goods in the intermediate position between the producer and the retailer. They purchase goods in large quantities and leave the division into small quantities to the retailer.

FUNCTIONS OF THE WHOLESALER

A wholesaler has a number of functions; the main ones are listed below.

(a) He removes from the manufacturer the burden of marketing his goods. He does this by purchasing large quantities from the manufacturer, thus clearing the assembly line and removing from the manufacturer the need for large storehouses. He pays promptly for all goods purchased, thus assisting further production.

(b) He assumes the risk of the enterprise begun by manufacturer, e.g. that goods produced would not be sold, or if sold, go at a lower price than that at which they were bought.

(c) He warehouses goods in such a way as to prevent deterioration and theft.

(d) He transports goods from point of production to warehouses and to retailers.

(e) He markets the goods by advertising, displays and demonstrations. He may package, blend and brand where necessary.

(f) He grants credit to retailers whose resources are limited.

(g) He acts as liaison between retailers and producers.

(h) He evens out the flow of goods in time of glut or shortage by taking supplies from stock or releasing them into stock. This function maintains price stability.

TYPES OF WHOLESALERS

(a) Large general wholesalers operating very large warehouses.

(b) Specialist wholesalers operating in a limited field.

(c) Cash and carry warehouses operating in the cut-price groceries and general retailing fields.

(d) Mail order wholesalers.

Questions

1 Distinguish between home trade and foreign trade.

2 Make a list of the different types of retailers found in your country, under the following headings: small scale with shops; small scale without shops; large scale.

3 Give the difference in functions between a retailer and a wholesaler.

4 Distinguish between a supermarket, a department store, and a variety chain store.

5 What is mail order selling?

11 Price determination

Supply and demand

In Chapter 4 when we looked at economic systems we saw that, under capitalism or in a free market system, the questions of what to produce, how much, for whom, by whom and by what methods are decided by the price mechanism.

The price mechanism is the system which rations out scarce resources among competing ends.

How does the price mechanism work?

In an earlier chapter we said that people have wants or desires. These wants are translated into demand by people's willingness and ability to pay the price for a given commodity. In other words, people show their preference for an article by their willingness to pay the going price.

We usually define the demand for a commodity as the quantity of that commodity which people are willing to purchase at the going price over a period of time. We can then draw up a demand schedule for a commodity. The demand schedule shows the quantity of the commodity which will be purchased over a given range of prices.

Price per unit ($)	Quantity demanded (thousands per week)
60	0
50	1
40	2
30	3
20	4
10	5

Demand schedule

An examination of the schedule shows that the lower the price of a commodity, then the more people will buy and vice versa. This same information can be shown diagramatically, e.g.

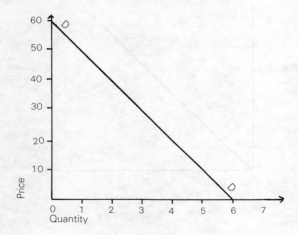

Demand curve

The line DD is called the demand curve and normally it would slope downwards from left to right showing that as price decreases more of the product is demanded. The other side of the picture is the supply side. Supply is the quantity of a commodity or service which producers or manufacturers are prepared to offer for sale at the going price. Note that both demand and supply depend on price.

We can draw up a supply schedule to show the quantity of a commodity that would be offered for sale at the going price.

Price per unit ($)	Quantity supplied (thousands per week)
60	6
50	5
40	4
30	3
20	2
10	1

Supply schedule

Here we see that suppliers can only be coaxed to offer more for sale

79

by higher prices. In other words, the higher the price, the more would be offered for sale. Again this can be shown diagramatically.

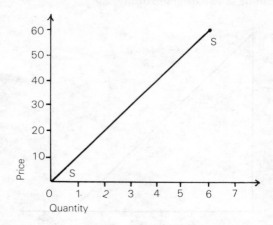

Supply curve

The line SS is the supply curve, and normally slopes upwards from left to right, showing that the greater the price, the greater the amount supplied.

If we now put the two curves together, we see this result.

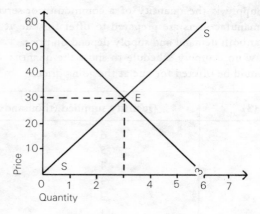

Supply and demand

At the price of $30.00 three thousand units of the commodities would be demanded by consumers, and three thousand would be offered for sale by suppliers. The market is therefore cleared. If the price were higher, say $40.00, suppliers would offer four thousand units for sale but consumers would only be willing to purchase two thousand, there would be an excess of supply over demand and the price would therefore fall back to $30.00. If the price were $20.00, consumers would be demanding four thousand units, but suppliers would only be supplying two thousand. Demand would exceed supply, forcing the price up to $30.00, which is said to be the equilibrium price, i.e. the price tends to settle at that level at which demand is equal to supply.

Value, price and opportunity cost

In modern economies, value means the significance of an article or its utility, or exchange power: i.e. how much one is willing to sacrifice to have the commodity or service. This exchange can be expressed in monetary terms by price. Price is thus the exchange value of a good measured in terms of money. For example the value of a new car is not the amount of labour which went into making it, nor is it the cost of producing it, but the amount of money one is willing to sacrifice to have the new car.

Value is related to cost from the point of view of opportunity cost or real cost: i.e. the sacrifice made to obtain a commodity. For example, what is the real cost to a man of building a home? It is the vacations lost to him and his family, or the new car he did not purchase, or the sacrifice of savings. In other words the real cost or value of a commodity is not just the money spent on the commodity (the price), but all the other things that were sacrificed in order to purchase the commodity.

Fixed and variable costs

The production of any commodity involves cost, e.g. cost of raw materials, labour, buildings, etc. Cost can be divided into two parts: (i) fixed, or supplementary costs; (ii) variable, or prime costs.

Fixed costs (overheads) are costs which are independent of the quantity produced, and do not alter as the output of the firm varies. Such fixed costs include administration, rents and rates and interest on the original capital borrowed.

Variable costs are additional costs and vary with output. They are the cost of labour, fuel and raw materials and the cost of maintenance and repairing of equipment.

Fixed costs only alter in the long-run when more capital and labour is used, but the variable costs change in both the short-run and long-run. They increase as production increases.

Perfect and imperfect competition

In economics and business a market is the system which brings buyers and sellers in close contact. The market need not be localised in the sense of a physical presence at a given place. The contact may be either direct or through dealers. What is important is that the prices obtained in one part of the market affect the prices paid in other parts. Thus we can speak of a regional market and a world market.

Markets may be either perfect or imperfect. A perfect market is one with the following characteristics:

(a) there must be many buyers and sellers, each one being too small to exert any influence on the price;
(b) the commodity must be homogeneous;
(c) there must be perfect knowledge as regards price;
(d) there must exist a single price for the commodity.

PERFECT COMPETITION

A perfect market is generally associated with perfect competition. Under perfect competition the same characteristics hold as for a perfect market. No seller can influence price as he represents too small a proportion of total supplies. Price is governed by forces over which individual suppliers and buyers have no influence: buyers and sellers are price takers.

The position can be shown diagramatically like this.

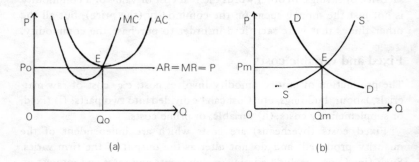

(a)   (b)

(a)   *Firm's equilibrium position*
(b)   *Industry's equilibrium position*

In order to explain the diagram we must first introduce some new concepts. The curve AC is the average cost curve and represents the average costs to the producer for producing a given range of output. Average cost is total cost divided by the number of units produced. MC is the marginal cost and represents costs for producing an additional unit of output. AR refers to the average revenue curve. Average revenue is total revenue divided by the number of units sold. The average revenue curve usually represents the demand curve and gives an indication of the price. MR refers to marginal revenue and represents the increase in total returns resulting from the sale of an additional unit.

Under perfect competition average returns equal marginal returns since there is one price for all units sold, and they are represented by a horizontal line. The average cost and marginal cost curves are U-shaped. This is a result of the law of variable proportions. The curves are falling when increasing returns are being experienced, and rising when returns begin to decrease. Under perfect competition the firm will be in equilibrium where its average cost is at its lowest; at that point only will the horizontal demand curve be tangent to the bottom of the average cost curve. It is also at that point that both marginal costs and average costs will be equal. If price is above that point and if the producer continues production to the right of that point he will be making a loss. If at this point average cost were to exceed average revenue the firm would go out of business.

IMPERFECT COMPETITION

An imperfect market is one where buyers and sellers do not possess perfect knowledge about prices charged elsewhere and where goods offered for sale are not homogeneous but have some differentiating quality, real or unreal. Thus price differences exist.

Monopoly

A pure monopoly exists where there is only one supplier of a certain commodity or group of substitutes. If there is one buyer we have a monopolist who can determine the price at which he is going to sell, however he cannot fix both price and quantity supplied. The aim of the monopolist is to maximise his profit: he fixes prices at a level that will give him the highest possible profit.

Price under pure monopoly

Under pure monopoly the average revenue curve is no longer a horizontal line, but slopes downwards from left to right. This indicates that the monopolist can only increase his sales if he is prepared to drop his price. The monopolist like the perfect competitor will determine his output by the intersection of his marginal revenue and marginal cost curves (G in the diagram). This point also indicates the position where the difference between average cost and average revenue is greatest. This means that monopoly profit (ABEF) is at its maximum. The monopolist could produce more than OD without incurring a loss but

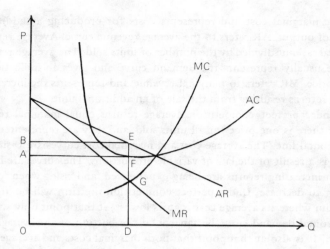

Price under pure monopoly

his monopoly profit would be less. The monopolist is earning more than normal profits, represented by the difference between his total revenue (ODEB) and his total outlay (ODFA).

Disadvantages of monopoly

(a) Prices tend to be higher than under a competitive system.
(b) Prices tend to be rigid and not influenced by changes in demand.
(c) It gives considerable power to the monopolist who wields it over his employees and his customers. In a democracy monopoly power is undesirable.
(d) Monopoly tends to breed monopoly.
(e) The monopolist tends to be complacent and production might be inefficient. There is also excess capacity in the plant.

OTHER EXAMPLES OF IMPERFECT COMPETITION

In the real world perfect competition or pure monopoly is rarely found. There are always some sellers or buyers who account for a significantly large proportion of total supply or sales to be able to influence price. No seller enjoys an absolute monopoly (except in some utilities) because substitutes can always be found. Goods are not (with few exceptions) perfectly homogeneous, and individual buyers will always prefer the products of one seller to those of another. Each seller therefore enjoys a partial monopoly. We thus have, in real life, elements of both competition and monopoly. Each seller tries to create for himself a partial advantage of monopoly in order to sell his product at a slightly higher price without having to fear that he will at once be outbid by his competitors. Thus we find in imperfect competition such things as branding of goods, advertising, specials and other sales gimmicks.

Duopoly and Oligopoly

Duopoly is the situation where two sellers of a product dominate the market. This happens occasionally, for example, where a couple of steel makers or a couple of railroads dominate the market in a particular country. Oligopoly is the more common case where a few sellers dominate the market. In oligopoly we have a few sellers producing almost homogeneous products. Prices under oligopoly tend to be rigid: the few companies all end up charging the same price for their products. This is done to prevent price rivalry and competition is shifted away from prices into areas such as advertising, changing the wrapping of the products and the size of their replacement parts, and in providing quick and reliable service.

The equilibrium position of firms operating under a system of oligopoly resembles that shown for a monopolist.

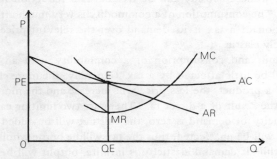

Price determination under imperfect competition in the long run

Cartels

A cartel is an organisation of a number of producers for the common selling of their products. In a cartel the title of the commodity passes from the hands of the individual producer into those of the cartel itself. The individual producer however retains his individuality as a unit of production and enterprise. Cartels are common in both industry and agriculture. Cartels can earn and maintain monopoly profits only if they can restrict the production of their members without interfering too much with their independence of management.

If there is no control or rationing of individual producers, the cartel can lead to individual producers increasing their production. However with no restrictions of entry and no rationing of production the cartel cannot, in the long run, give members above normal profits. If the cartel succeeds in raising prices to the point where profit is abnormally high in the industry new firms will enter the industry, and production will increase, leading to a fall in prices and in the level of profits. Therefore if the cartel wants to obtain monopoly prices for its product it must be able to both ration the production of its members by quotas and restrict entry into the industry.

The effect of government price regulations

Due to imperfections in the workings of the price system, governments are forced to intervene from time to time to minimise the results of these imperfections. There are basically two methods used by governments when intervention is considered necessary. These are: (i) the manipulation of market prices through taxation or subsidies; (ii) the control of demand through rationing.

The imposition of a tax can be treated as an increase in the cost of production, while a subsidy can be treated as a reduction in cost of production. The consumption of a commodity is very much affected by the imposition of a tax if its demand over the relevant price range is comparatively elastic.

The output and consumption of a commodity with an inelastic demand will be little affected by a tax. Generally, the more elastic the demand for a product, the less price will increase and the more output will fall as the result of a direct tax. There are two limiting cases here: where elasticity of demand is zero, the full tax will be added to price and output will be unaffected, thus the tax will be borne wholly by the producer, while if demand elasticity is infinite, output will be reduced to zero.

On the supply side, if a commodity is produced under conditions of increasing costs, the long-run increase in price caused by the tax will be affected to some extent by the lower costs of production as output falls. On the other hand, if decreasing costs conditions exist, price will tend to rise by more than the tax, since average costs of production will increase with falling output.

Rationing is an attempt to influence production and consumption by regulating the demand at any given price. If a commodity is in short supply the price will normally be driven up. Rationing attempts to match demand to supply, thus moderating the rise in prices. In this way the shortage does not result in the relatively poor member of the community being pushed out of the market by the relatively rich. Rationing has several disadvantages.

(a) It may require a large amount of labour and other resources to administer it.

(b) The principle of free choice is contravened.

(c) It creates the establishment of illegal trading, e.g. 'black market'.

(d) It impedes the normal forces of adjustment in the market taking place.

Profit

Mr Jones converts the lower floor of his house into a grocery shop. He stocks it with $5,000.00 worth of goods, and runs it himself. At the end of the year Mr Jones finds that total sales or turnover amount to $8,000.00, which means that he earned a return of $3,000.00 in profit. However, an economist would ask, how much of the $3,000.00 should be regarded as the return due to labour (what Mr Jones would have earned if he had been employed by someone else); how much should be regarded as interest (the money which Mr Jones would have received if he had lent out his money at the going interest rate); how much should be imputed for rent (the amount of money which Mr Jones would have earned from letting his premises to someone else). Only after these imputed charges have been considered can one speak of profit in the economic sense: pure profit, which is actual profit minus personal wages, interest and rent.

From the above we see that profit is the reward for entrepreneurial services, i.e. for risk bearing. It is a residue of what is left over after certain charges have been taken out. Profits can be expressed either as a sum of money, e.g. $3,000.00, or as a profit rate as a percentage on the capital employed in the business, as it is the turning over of the capital which accounts for the sales of the firm and thus for the profits.

e.g. $\dfrac{\text{Gross profit}}{\text{Capital}} \times 100$ = percentage profit rate.

In our example, $\dfrac{\$3000}{\$5000} \times \dfrac{100}{1} = 60\%$

Gross profit may also be expressed as a percentage of turnover.

i.e. $\dfrac{\text{Gross profit}}{\text{Turnover}} \times \dfrac{100\%}{1}$

Turnover and stock return

Turnover is the total value of sales. Stock turn refers to the speed or rate of transactions or sales. In simple terms it is the number of times the stock is turned over in the course of a week, month or year. The stock turn or rate of stock turnover is measured by dividing net sales by the average stock value at selling price, or by dividing the cost price of goods sold by the average stock value at cost price. e.g.

$$\text{Stock turn} = \frac{\text{Net sales}}{\text{Average stock at selling price}}$$

or

$$\frac{\text{Cost of sales}}{\text{Average stock at cost price}}$$

$$\text{Average} = \frac{\text{Value of stock at beginning of period + value of stock at end of period}}{2}$$

Questions

1 Explain the workings of the price mechanism.
2 How is equilibrium reached in the markets?
3 Distinguish between fixed cost and variable cost.
4 What are the chief characteristics of (i) perfect competition; (ii) imperfect competition; (iii) pure monopoly?
5 Distinguish between accounting and economic profit.

12 Documents used in home trade

In this chapter we shall consider some of the documents, terms and methods of payments used in the world of trade and business.

Documents used in trade

The use of documents in trade is very important. Documents allow the trader or businessman to keep records of transactions, e.g. the amount of goods sold and to whom. They also supply him with information such as suppliers of commodities, type of commodities (style, size, etc.) and price listings. Finally, documents provide information for his accounting system, i.e. his credit and debit position.

During the course of a year the businessman may use several different types of documents. Here are some of the most common ones and their use.

LETTER OF ENQUIRY
A businessman (trader or retailer) ordering goods for the first time from a wholesaler or manufacturer, would write a letter of enquiry, requesting information about the type and class of goods required, and asking for a quotation (or a price list). He would also ask for details of the supplier's terms of trading, and the availability of stocks. For example, would the goods be supplied from stock or would there be a waiting period, and if there was a delay, how much of a delay?

The businessman will need to set out all his queries clearly, so that the supplier knows exactly what is required.

```
┌─────────────────────────────────────────────────────────────────┐
│                          ENQUIRY                                  │
│                                                                   │
│   PHONE NO: 89852                      Ian Cudjoe & Co. Ltd.,     │
│                                        Oistins,                   │
│                                        Christ Church,             │
│                                        Barbados,                  │
│                                        24th June, 19--            │
│                                                                   │
│   The Manager,                                                    │
│   Crescent Metal Works,                                           │
│   Eastern Main Road,                                              │
│   Trinidad.                                                       │
│                                                                   │
│   Dear Sir,                                                       │
│                                                                   │
│      We should be obliged if you would forward to us an illustrated │
│   catalogue of your metal furniture, together with a price list, and │
│   a statement of the terms upon which we can be supplied.         │
│                                                                   │
│      As we need certain lines of furniture for the coming Christmas │
│   season, we should be grateful if you would inform us whether the │
│   furniture can be supplied immediately from stock.               │
│                                                                   │
│                                        Yours faithfully,          │
│                                                                   │
│                                        I. Cudjoe                  │
│                                        Director                   │
└─────────────────────────────────────────────────────────────────┘
```

Letter of enquiry

COVERING LETTER
The manufacturer, on receiving the letter of enquiry from a potential
customer, would forward the catalogue and price list requested, together
with a covering letter. The price list would give the reference numbers
and the prices of all the items shown in the catalogue. He would also
answer any queries about his terms of trading and the availability of
stocks. As he will wish to attract custom, he will be as helpful as he can.

Crescent Metal Works,
Eastern Main Road,
Trinidad.
1st July, 19--.

Ian Cudjoe & Co. Ltd.,
Oistins,
Christ Church,
Barbados.

Dear Sirs,

Thank you for your enquiry of 24th June. I have pleasure in enclosing a copy of our latest catalogue together with a copy of the current price list.

Terms of payment are: 10% discount for cash or 90 days bill of exchange. Carriage is paid on all orders above $2,000.

Delivery can be made from stock and I can assure you of immediate attention at all times.

I look forward to receiving your order at an early date.

Yours faithfully,

. . . .

J. Merchant
Crescent Metal Works
Manager.

Covering letter

```
┌─────────────────────────────────────────────────────────────┐
│                    ORDER              No.  14                 │
│                                                               │
│                              Ian Cudjoe & Co. Ltd.,           │
│                              Oistins,                         │
│                              Christ Church,                   │
│                              Barbados.                        │
│                                                               │
│                              7th July, 19--                   │
│                                                               │
│   Crescent Metal Works,                                       │
│   Eastern Main Road,                                          │
│   Trinidad.                                                   │
│                                                               │
│   Please supply:                                              │
│   Catalogue                                                   │
│   Reference                                                   │
│   871 - 011 - 3   1 dozen wrought iron 5 piece dinette sets at│
│                      $250.00 each                             │
│                                                               │
│   Catalogue                                                   │
│   Reference                                                   │
│   861 - 217 - 8   1 dozen wrought iron 3 piece living room suites│
│                      at $300.00 each                          │
│                                                               │
│   Delivery within 14 days.                                    │
│                                                               │
│                                    I. Cudjoe.                 │
└─────────────────────────────────────────────────────────────┘
```

Order form

THE ORDER

When a customer decides to place an order with a supplier, he may place his order in writing in a letter or by using his firm's own order forms.

When the order is made out, the original copy goes to the supplier, one copy is sent to the storehouse to check against the goods when they are received, and the third copy is retained by the order department to check against the supplier's invoice when that is forwarded.

Note that the order has a reference number and gives a full description of the goods ordered and also the degree of urgency.

```
+-------------------------------------------------------------+
| INVOICE NO: 44                  Crescent Metal Works,       |
|                                 Eastern Main Road,          |
|                                 Trinidad.                   |
|                                                             |
| Ian Cudjoe & Co. Ltd.,                                      |
| Oistins,                        14th July, 19--             |
| Christ Church,                                              |
| Barbados                                                    |
|                                                             |
| Bought of                                                   |
|                                                             |
| Crescent Metal Works,                                       |
| Eastern Main Road,                                          |
| Trinidad                                                    |
|                                                             |
| Ref your order no. 14                                       |
|                                                    $  .  ¢  |
| Ref. No.       1 dozen wrought iron 5-piece                 |
| 871-011-3      dinette sets @ $250.00            3000 . 00  |
|                                                             |
| Ref. No.                                                    |
| 861-217-8      1 dozen wrought iron 3-piece living          |
|                room suites @ $300.00             3600 . 00  |
|                                                  --------   |
|                Total                             6600 . 00  |
|                                                             |
| E & O.E.                                                    |
+-------------------------------------------------------------+
```

Invoice

THE INVOICE

Having made enquiries and satisfied himself that the customer is a trust-
worthy firm, the supplier would prepare the goods for delivery. As in
our example, it is an overseas sale, J. Merchant would not send an
advice or delivery note, the purpose of which is to identify the goods
ordered without showing the price, but would despatch his official
invoice.

The invoice is a bill sent by the supplier to the purchaser immediately after the goods have been despatched. It contains all details of the
purchase: quantity, type, grade, price, etc, with trade discount deducted
from the price, if it applies. Five copies of the invoice will be made out,
each in a different colour. One copy goes to the customer, another to
the sales department, another to the accounts department, one is a

despatch copy for traffic (storehouse) and finally one is used as an advice/delivery note. Copies used as advice/delivery notes will not include prices.

When Ian Cudjoe receives the invoice, he will check it with his copy of the order form, and when the goods arrive they will also be checked with the order.

E & O.E. on the bottom of the invoice means 'errors and omissions excepted'. If an error or omission has been made the firm supplying the goods will put it right.

THE CREDIT NOTE

Suppose that either an overcharge has been made, say for example, the supplier's typist typed the total as $7,600.00 instead of $6,600.00, or that some damage was done to the goods in transit, for which the manufacturer has agreed to accept responsibility. He will then send the customer a credit note in cancellation of part of the original invoice. The credit note, printed in red, is also used to adjust accounts between debtor and creditor for returned 'empties'. The opposite of a credit note is a debit note. It is used to add amounts to the original invoice, e.g. an undercharge or omission.

```
-----------------------------------------------------------------

   CREDIT NOTE No. NP.1                        Ian Cudjoe,
                                               Oistins,
                                               Christ Church,
                                               Barbados.

                        Credited by
                        Crescent Metal Works,
                        Eastern Main Road,
                        Trinidad.

                                                 21st July, 19--
    Catalogue
    Reference                                       $  .  ¢
    871-011-3      4 chairs from dinette set
                   @ $25.00 each                    100 . 00

    861-217-8      2 3-piece wrought iron living
                   room suites @ $300.00
                   Returned damaged                 600 . 00
                                                   ---------
                                                    700 . 00
-----------------------------------------------------------------
```

Credit note

94

```
┌─────────────────────────────────────────────────────────────┐
│                                                               │
│                        STATEMENT                              │
│                                                               │
│                              Crescent Metal Works,            │
│                              Eastern Main Road,               │
│                              Trinidad.                        │
│                                                               │
│                              31st August, 19--                │
│                                                               │
│   Ian Cudjoe & Co. Ltd.,                                      │
│   Oistins,                                                    │
│   Christ Church,                                              │
│   Barbados.                                                   │
│                                                               │
│   Date          Particulars              $ . ¢               │
│   19--                                                        │
│   July  14      Invoice No.  44          6600 . 00           │
│         28      Invoice No.  58          7000 . 00           │
│   Aug.  11      Invoice No.  99          4560 . 00           │
│         30      Invoice No. 145          3330 . 00           │
│                                          ─────────            │
│                 Less                     21490 . 00          │
│   July  21      Credit No.  1             700 . 00           │
│   Aug.  15      Credit No. 12             800 . 00           │
│                                          ─────────            │
│                                          19990 . 00          │
│                                          ─────────            │
│   E & O.E.      Terms: 10% one month                          │
└─────────────────────────────────────────────────────────────┘
```

Statement

THE STATEMENT

Suppose that the transactions between Ian Cudjoe & Co. Ltd. and
Crescent Metal Works were done on a credit basis, and that Ian Cudjoe
& Co. Ltd. placed several orders during a particular time period, say one
month or a quarter, with Crescent Metal Works. With each delivery of
furniture the manufacturer would send an invoice. At the end of the
account period the accounts department of Crescent Metal Works would
send a statement to Ian Cudjoe & Co. Ltd. showing the total indebtedness, or amounts owing, on the transactions. Ian Cudjoe & Co. Ltd. will
check this statement with the invoices which they have received, allowances being made for credit and debit notes in connection with the
transactions.

Ian Cudjoe & Co. Ltd. would then send a bank draft or use some other method of payment to settle their account with Crescent Metal Works.

The statement also shows the terms of payment. Notice that at the bottom it states '10% one month'. This indicates to Ian Cudjoe & Co. Ltd. that if they settle their debt with Crescent Metal Works within one month they will receive a 10% cash discount. In some cases the purchaser may also receive a trade discount. A cash discount is given to debtors who pay promptly for their goods when the time for payment has arrived.

Trade discount is a reduction in the catalogue price of an article, given by the manufacturer or the wholesaler to the retailer, to enable him to make a profit.

RECEIPT
A receipt is given for cash payment, but is not required if payment has been made by cheque or bank draft, as these furnish evidence of payment.

The examples given here dealt mainly with regional trade. For home and extra-regional trade, the procedure may vary. In home trade, we may use advice notes and consignment notes and where credit is to be given, a status enquiry would first have to be made.

Some other terms used in trade

C/PD   Carriage paid.

F.O.B.   Free on board. All expenses up to and including putting the goods on board the ship are included, but expenses of shipment, customs and dock dues at the destination port are excluded.

C.I.F.   Cost, insurance and freight. This includes all costs and expenses to the port of destination.

F.A.S.   Free alongside ship. The quoted price only includes expenses and delivery to the docks. Loading charges onto the ship are not included.

Certificate of origin   This is a certificate of declaration, issued by the exporter in the country of origin, of the goods he is shipping. It is required to determine any preferential tariff rates which might apply, e.g. duty free entry of Caricom goods.

Certificate of inspection   This is a health certificate and applies mainly to foodstuffs such as meat and fruit. The produce is certified to be in a consumable condition and free from contamination.

C/F   Carriage forward. Expenses are to be paid from a stated place, e.g. shop or factory, by the purchaser.

Loco   Purchaser to pay carriage from a stated place.

Franco   All carriage charges are paid by the seller to the purchaser's address.

F.O.R.   Free on rail. Carriage will be paid, by the vendor, to the nearest railway station.

Bill of lading   This represents the title to the goods while they are on the high seas; ownership of the goods is transferred to the purchaser. It is a receipt for the goods shipped, evidence of the contract of carriage, and the document of title.

The shipping note   This note is submitted to the Port Authority who receives the goods for shipping. It tells them what goods are being handed into their care and the ship they are to be loaded on to.

The airway bill   Every consignment of goods by air must be covered by an airway bill in three parts:

Part one   'For the carrier' and signed by the consignor.

Part two   'For the consignee' and travels with the goods. It is signed by both the carrier and consignor.

Part three is signed by the carrier and returned to the consignor.

All goods imported or exported must be passed by customs officials. Printed forms must be completed to show the type of merchandise and its liability for duty, details of the shipment and the source of origin of the goods.

Methods of payment

Trade, we said earlier, is the exchange of goods between buyers and sellers at an agreed price. This means that commodities bought and sold both locally and overseas must be paid for. Several methods of payment have been established in order to facilitate trade. The actual method used would depend on the following factors:

(a) The amount: how large a sum must be paid.

(b) The distance (in terms of space): if the money is to be sent some distance, a representation of money will become necessary.

(c) Safety: this is an important consideration where money is to be sent abroad, through the port.

(d) Date when due: if payment is due in the future a promissory note or bill of exchange may be required.

(e) Urgency: how urgently is payment required? The answer to this may require the use of some special medium to transmit the message authorising the payment.

(f) Does the debtor have a bank account? It is important for the debtor to have the type of account which would facilitate easy payment.

97

NOTES, COINS AND CHEQUES

For small amounts, coins may be used, e.g. in the purchase of goods over the counter, or to make up odd amounts in larger sums of money. For larger sums bank-notes issued by the Central Bank are generally used, since they are legal tender for any amount of money. Bank-notes may also be sent through the post. In practice, however, rather than large quantities of bank-notes, cheques are generally used by traders and businessmen, in both the retail and wholesale trade.

If money is to be sent some distance, either locally or overseas, it is better to use some representation of money. There are several such representations which can be used. For example, locally, as we have seen above, a cheque may be used. We may also use a Postal Order, issued by the Post Office for varying amounts up to a specific sum. A Postal Order is an issued blank, and the sender must fill in the name of the payee and the office of payment before posting the order. Postal Orders may be crossed like a cheque to make sure that payment is made only through a bank.

When making overseas payments there are several methods we may use. For example, we may use the Postal Order mentioned above, or we may use Money Orders. The Post Office transact Money Order business by issuing orders up to a maximum sum. In filling out a Money Order form, the sender must state:

(a) the amount of the order;   (d) the name and address of payee;
(b) in which currency;   (e) the name and address of the sender.
(c) where payable;

The sender receives a Money Order which he remits to the payee. Both Postal Orders and Money Orders have limited use in international trade.

Other methods of making overseas payments are:

(a) Telegraphic Money Orders. Here the issuing Post Office sends a telegram of advice to the paying office. The sender must pay a small supplementary fee for this service. Banks also remit money by telegraphic orders or by telephone.

(b) Bankers' Drafts. There are two main types.

 (i) Sight draft. This is simply a cheque drawn on a foreign bank (or an overseas branch of a local bank). Where payment is to be by sight draft the exporter sends the documents of title (bill of lading) to the importer's bank, the bank handing over the documents against payment.

 (ii) Bill of exchange. This is 'an unconditional order in writing, addressed by one person to another, signed by the person giving it, requiring the person to whom it is addressed to pay

Shipped

in and upon the good ship called the .... Master of this present Voyage, and now riding

wheref ....

at anchor in CARLISLE BAY, BRIDGETOWN, bound for ....

MARKS

being marked and numbered as in the margin, and are to be delivered in the like good order

and well-conditioned at the aforesaid Port of ....

(the Act of God, the Queen's Enemies, Fire and all and every other the Dangers and Accidents

of the Seas, Rivers, and Navigation of whatsoever nature and kind soever excepted) unto

....

or to .... Assigns. Freight for the said goods to be paid in

....

....

Primage and Average accustomed.

In Witness whereof, the Master or Purser of the said ship hath affirmed to .... Bills

of Lading, all of this Tenor and Date, the one of which Bills being accomplished, the others

to stand void.

BARBADOS this .... 19 ....

....

Master

Local shipping document

BARBADOS

BILL OF SIGHT

Form C. 12 — Customs,
Reg. 31

Declaration under Section 38 of the Customs Act, 1962

No. of Bill of Lading ....

Port of Importation ....

Importer's Name ....

Name of Aircraft or Ship	Master's/Commander's Name	Date of Report	Port or Place whence arrived

Marks and Numbers	Number and Description of Packages, with such information as the Importer is able to give as to Quantity and Value of Goods
....	....
....	....
....	....
....	....
....	....
....	....
....	....
....	....
....	....
....	....
....	....
....	....
....	....
....	....
....	....

I, ... the Importer, or

.... Agent of the Importer,
of the Goods above-mentioned, do hereby declare that I have not, and that to the best of my knowledge he has not received sufficient
Invoice, Bill of Lading, or other advice from which the Quantity, Quality or Value of the Goods above-mentioned, can be ascertained.

Dated this..day of..19..................

....
Witness   *Importer or Agent* (1)

Declared before me this..day of..19....................

....
for Comptroller of Customs

NOTE: (1) The Importer or his Agent may examine the above-mentioned goods for the purposes of making entry according to law.
            (2) The declaration and signature of the Importer or his Agent must be attested by the proper Officer, or by a witness whose signature is
                  known to, and who is approved by the Comptroller.

Printed by Barbados Government Printing Office.

Bill of sight (for imported goods other than goods in transit or for transhipment)

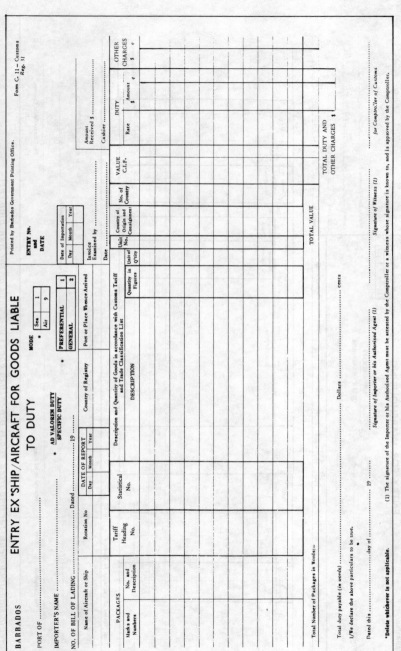

Import bill (for goods liable to duty)

BARBADOS

ENTRY FOR WAREHOUSING

Form C.13 – Customs
Reg. 31

MODE * Sea 1 / Air 9

PORT OF ....

IMPORTER'S NAME ....

NO. OF BILL OF LADING .... Dated ....19..........

Ex* .... SHIP/AIRCRAFT
.... QUEEN'S WAREHOUSE
*Delete whichever is not applicable.

Amount Rent Received $ ....

Cashier .... Date. ....

Cash Book No. ....

Invoice No. .... Exd. By.................. Date ....

Name of Aircraft or Ship	Rotation No.	Date of Report			Country of Registry	Port or Place whence Arrived
		Day	Mth.	Year		

Description and Quantity of Goods in Accordance with Customs Tariff and Trade Classification List

Warehouse Register		Particulars of Warehousing		PACKAGES		Tariff Heading No.	Statistical No.	DESCRIPTION	Quantity in figures	Unit of Qt'ty	Unit No.	Country of Origin and Consignment	No. of Country	VALUE C.I.F $ ¢
No.	Page	B/E or W/E	Date	Marks and Numbers	No. and Description									

Total Number of Packages in Words:—

TOTAL VALUE $.

Warehouse Rent Assessed Overleaf
$

I/We declare the above particulars to be true and enter the above mentioned goods

for Warehousing in .... warehouse at .... at a value of (in words)

Date .... 19 ....
.... Dollars .... cents. Dated this .... day of .... 19 ....

Officer i/c ....
Warehouse A/c ....

.... For Comptroller. Date
.... Importer or his Agent.

.... For Comptroller of Customs.

Warehousing document (for imported goods other than goods in transit or for transhipment)

| EXAMINATIONS | Goods stored in the Queen's Warehouse | RELEASES AND RECEIPTS |

Delivery Order

To the Queen's Warehousekeeper at ....

Please deliver to .... the packages

entered overleaf, ... Agent

.... 19 ....

RENT

From .... to .... inclusive ....

PACKAGES		Measurement	No. of periods	Rate per period	Amount
Nos.	No. of				
				TOTAL	

....

....

Officer I/c Warehouse Accounts

.... 19 ....

103

ENTRY FOR GOODS FREE OF DUTY

Form C. 10 — Customs
Reg. 31

BARBADOS

PORT OF ....

DELIVERED ....

* EX QUEEN'S [1]   GOVERNMENT [2]   PRIVATE WAREHOUSE [3]   PRIVATE MANUFACTURING [4]

ENTRY NO. and DATE

IMPORTER'S NAME .... Dated .... 19 ....

*AIRCRAFT EX SHIP [0]

MODE * Sea [1] Air [9]

NO. OF BILL OF LADING .... 19 ....

Date of Importation
| Day | Month | Year |

NAME OF WAREHOUSE ....

Name of Aircraft or Ship	Rotation No. of Aircraft or Ship	Date of Report			Country of Registry	Port or Place whence Arrived	Date Warehoused		
		Day	Mth.	Year			Day	Mth.	Year

Invoice Examined by ....

Date ....

PARTICULARS OF WAREHOUSING

Rotation No.	Book No.	Folio No.	W/E or F/W No.	Date	PACKAGES		TARIFF HEADING No.	STATIS-TICAL No.	Description and Quantity of Goods in accordance with combined Customs Tariff and Trade Classification List				Country of Origin and Consignment	No. of Country	VALUE C.I.F.	
					Marks and Numbers	No. and Description			DESCRIPTION	Quantity in Figures	Unit of Qtity	Unit No.			$	¢

TOTAL

Warehouse Rent Assessed Overleaf

Amount Rent Received $ ....

Cashier ....

**Goods entering the Island Free by reason of/for use of:—

Item No.		Item No.	
11 ☐		55 ☐	
12 ☐		67 ☐	
13 ☐		68 ☐	
24 ☐		75 ☐	
25 ☐		76 ☐	
36 ☐		77 ☐	
45 ☐		85 ☐	
46 ☐		99 ☐	

Total Number of Packages in Words:—

I/We enter the above Goods as Free of Duty and declare that the particulars set forth above are correctly stated.

Dated this .... day of .... 19 ....

....
Signature of Importer or his Authorised Agent (1)

*Delete whichever is not applicable.

....
Signature of Witness (1)

(1) The signature of the Importer or his Authorised Agent must be attested by the Comptroller or a Witness whose signature is known to and is approved by the Comptroller.

....
for Comptroller of Customs.

TOTAL PAYABLE

**See overleaf for what Code Nos. 11/99 indicate and show thus X in square for whichever is applicable.

Printed by Barbados Government Printing Office.

Document for duty-free goods (for imported goods other than goods in transit or for transhipment)

104

Goods stored in the Queen's* /Government* Warehouse

Delivery Order

To the Queen's* /Government* Warehouse-keeper at .... the packages

Please deliver to ....

entered overleaf.

....

Owner or his Authorised Agent,

.... 19 ....

RENT

From .... to .... inclusive

PACKAGES		Measurement	No. of periods	Rate per period	Amount	
Nos.	No. of				$	¢
					TOTAL	

*Delete whichever is not applicable.

....

Officer-in-Charge Warehouse Accounts.

.... 19 ....

RELEASES

EXAMINATIONS

Goods normally dutiable which are admitted free of duty for the following reasons or uses are to be ticked overleaf in the appropriate box as explained below:

Goods for the use in/of:—

The Central Government other than the Port Department	::	11
A Local Government	::	12
The Port Department	::	13
Pioneer Industries	::	24
Hotels under the Hotel Aids Act	::	25
The Natural Gas Corporation	::	36
The Barbados Telephone Co. Ltd.	::	45
Cable & Wireless (W.I.) Ltd., and International Aeradio Ltd.	::	46
Oil Companies	::	55
The manufacturing of Sugar and Rum	::	67
Agriculture, (N.F.S.)	::	68
The manufacturing of Tobacco and Cocoa	::	75
The processing of copra or its by-products	::	76
The manufacturing of Ice	::	77
Cultural, health, social and approved associations and charitable institutions	::	85
and		
Goods allowed free entry for any other reasons	::	99

Form C. 33 – Customs
Reg. 106

BARBADOS

SHIPPING BILL ex WAREHOUSE

For Goods for Exportation or use as Aircraft's/Ship's Stores

PORT OF ....

| EX QUEEN'S | 1 | GOVERNMENT | 2 | PRIVATE | 3 |
| EX PRIVATE MANUFACTURING | 4 | | | | |

| MODE | Sea | 1 |
| | Air | 9 |

WAREHOUSE

EXPORT No. and DATE

EXPORTER'S NAME ....

Name and Rotation No. of Importing Aircraft or Ship ....

NAME OF WAREHOUSE .... *Ex Queen's/Government Warehouse

DATE WAREHOUSED ....

* FOR EXPORTATION — 1
* For Aircraft/Ship's Stores/Bunkers — 2

Amount of Rent Received $ ....
Cashier ....
Date ....

Name of Aircraft or Ship	Country of Registry	Destination of Aircraft or Ship	Station where Lying	Destination of Goods	No. of Country

In the case of Aircraft's/Ship's Stores/Bunkers the Destination of the Goods and the No. of the Country is to be the Country of Registry of the Vessel/Aircraft.

Agent of Aircraft or Ship	PACKAGES		TARIFF HEADING No.	STATISTICAL No.	Description and Quantity of Goods in accordance with combined Customs Tariff and Trade Classification List			Country of Origin and Consignment	Unit No.	No. of Country	Value F.O.B. on Exportation $ ¢	Value C.I.F. on Importation $ ¢
	Marks and Numbers	No. and Description			DESCRIPTION	Quantity in Figures	Unit of Q'ty					

PARTICULARS OF WAREHOUSING

Rotation No.	Book No.	Folio No.	W/S or E/N No.	Date

Total Number of Packages in Words:— ....

TOTAL VALUE

Warehouse Rent Assessed Overleaf $

I/We declare the above-particulars true and request permission to remove

Officer i/c ....

By .... (Mode of conveyance) from .... 19 .... warehouse at .... (place) by virtue of

Warehouse A/cs .... *General/Particular Bond dated .... 19 .... in the sum of $ .... the above mentioned goods for

Date .... (a) exportation to .... or (b) use as "Aircraft/Ship's Stores. Dated this .... day of .... 19 ....

.... Signature of Exporter or his Authorised Agent (1). .... Signature of Witness (1). .... for Comptroller of Customs.

* Delete whichever is not applicable. (1) The declaration and signature of the Exporter or his Authorised Agent must be attested by the Comptroller or a witness whose signature is known to and is approved by the Comptroller.

Printed by Barbados Government Printing Office.

See reverse side.

Shipping bill (for exportation of goods or for goods used as aircraft/ship's stores)

Goods Stored in the Queen's* /Government* Warehouse
Delivery Order

To the Queen's* /Government* Warehouse Keeper at ....

Please deliver to .... the packages

entered over* af.

....
Signature of Owner or Authorised Agent.

* Queen's
* Government

WAREHOUSE RENT

From .... to .... inclusive

PACKAGES		Measurement	No. of periods	Rate per period	Amount
Nos.	No. of			$	$ ¢
			TOTAL ..		

....
Officer i/c Warehouse Accounts
.... 19 ....

Particulars of (a) release from the warehouse, (b) certificate of shipment and (c) receipt on board from the Master/Commander.

(a) Released .... packages
Number of
as overleaf.

(date).................. 19 ....

....
Warehouse Officer.

(b) Shipped .... packages
Number of
as overleaf.

at .... at .... a.m./p.m.
Station

(date).................. 19 ....

....
Shipping Officer.

(c) Received .... packages
Number of
as overleaf.

(date).................. 19 ....

....
Master/Commander.

*Delete whichever is not applicable.

I hereby certify that bond as stated overleaf

* is in force
* has been given

Amount to be debited against the General Bond

$ ....

....
Officer.
.... 19 ....

Particulars of examination before shipment

....
Shipping Officer.

Date .... 19 ....

Particulars of examination on board

....
Boarding Officer.

Date .... 19 ....

107

BARBADOS

Form C. 27—Customs
Regs. 90, 106, 110, 111

Shipping Bill for Goods Re-Exported *(Not) Liable to Export Duties

	Sea	1
*	Air	9

EXPORT No.
and
DATE

PORT OF ....

EXPORTER'S NAME ....

* DRAWBACK OF CUSTOMS DUTIES CLAIMED
  DRAWBACK OF CUSTOMS DUTIES NOT CLAIMED

* FOR EXPORTATION	1
* FOR AIRCRAFT/SHIP'S STORES/BUNKERS	2

Name of Aircraft or Ship	Agent of Aircraft or Ship	Country of Registry	Destination of Aircraft or Ship	Destination of Goods	No. of Country

In the case of Aircraft/Ship's Stores/Bunkers the Destination of the Country and the No. of the Country is to be the Country of Registry of the Vessel/Aircraft

PACKAGES		Tariff Heading No.	Statistical No.	Description and Quantity of Goods in accordance with combined Customs Tariff and Trade Classification List			Unit No.	Country of Origin and Consignment	No. of Country	Value F.O.B.	Amount of Drawback claimed	Export Duty
Marks and Numbers	No. and Description			DESCRIPTION	Quantity in figures	Unit of Q'tity				$ ¢	$ ¢	$ ¢
										TOTAL		

Total Number of Packages in Words:—

I/We declare the above particulars to be true.

Dated this .... day of .... 19 ......

....
Signature of Exporter or his Authorised Agent (1)

....
Signature of Witness (1)

N.B.:— If Drawback claimed (a) show original marks and numbers of packages.
(b) complete the reverse side of this form.
(c) submit form C. 26 with details of Drawback claimed together with this form.

(1) The declaration and signature of the Exporter or his Authorised Agent must be attested by the Comptroller or a witness whose signature is known to and is approved by the Comptroller.

*Delete whichever is not applicable.

....
for Comptroller of Customs.

See reverse side.

Printed by Barbados Government Printing Office.

Shipping bill (for re-exported goods)

Drawback of Customs Duties for Goods Exported

PORT OF ....

DRAWBACK NO. ....

EXPORTER'S NAME ....

....
Customs Officer.

Certified Vessel/Aircraft named overleaf cleared, goods on content/not on content*

....
Clearance Officer

I .... do hereby declare that the goods of which particulars are given overleaf are in the unbroken packages in which they were originally imported, have not deteriorated in quantity, quality, or value, that the duties claimed have been paid thereon, and that the particulars of importation given hereunder relate to the goods described overleaf and are true.

....
Signature of Exporter or his Authorised Agent.

Dated this .... day of .... 19 ......

....
Signature of Witness

....
for Comptroller of Customs.

Name of Aircraft or Ship on which imported	Date of Importation	Entry No. and Date Duty Paid	Quantity of goods entered	Value when entered $ ¢	Amount of duty paid $ ¢	By whom duty paid	Quantity for re-export	Value C.I.F. $ ¢	Amount of Drawback claimed $ ¢
							Total No. of packages in words		

Shipped .... packages as overleaf .... Received the packages mentioned overleaf

Number of .... on board ....

by .... at .... Station

at .... a.m./p.m.

Date .... 19 ......

Shipping Officer

Date .... 19 ......

*Master or Commander

Examined/seen on board .... packages

Number of

at .... a.m./p.m.

Date .... 19 ......

Customs Boarding Officer

NOTICE OF EXPORTATION UNDER GENERAL BOND

Port of .... 19 ......

I .... give notice that I intend to export on board the ship/aircraft .... bound for ....

by virtue of General Bond dated .... the goods described on the other side hereof to be landed there within .... days.

Bond in force

Date .... 19 ......

....
Signature of Exporter or his Authorised Agent.

....
for Comptroller of Customs

*Delete whichever is not applicable.

109

THE GEEST LINE (GEEST INDUSTRIES LTD.)

EXPORTER/SHIPPER (Bills of Lading in the name of)		Ins. Cert. No.	B/L No.
		Exporters Ref.	
		F/Agents Ref.	

| CONSIGNEE: | Notify |
| | |

BILL OF LADING

THE GEEST LINE
P.O. Box 2
A Shed, No.2 Dock,
BARRY, South Glamorgan
CS6 6XP
Telephone: BARRY (0446) 732333
Telex: 49428

Ocean Vessel	Port of Loading		
Port of Discharge	Final Destination		No. of original Bs./L
Marks & Numbers	Numbers & kind of packages & description of Goods		Gross Weight Kilos	Cube Cu. Mtr.

Total No. of Packages (In Words)

Goods of a dangerous or damaging nature must not be tendered for shipment unless written notice of their nature and the name and address of the Sender have been previously given to the Carrier, Master or Agent of the vessel and the nature is distinctly marked on the outside of the package or packages as required by statute. A special stowage order giving consent to shipment must also be obtained from the Carrier.
Any lift weighting over two tons gross must be declared in writing before shipment and the weight be stancilled clearly on the package.
SHIPPED in apparent good order and condition unless otherwise stated and to be discharged at the aforesaid port of discharge or so near thereto as the vessel may safely get and be always afloat.
Weight, measure, marks, numbers, quality, contents of value, if mentioned in the Bill of Lading, are to be considered unknown unless the contary has been expressly acknowledged and agreed to. The signing of this Bill of Lading, is not to be considered as such an agreement.
In accepting this Bill of Lading the Merchant expressly accepts and agrees to all its stipulations, exceptions and conditions, on both pages, whether written printed, stamped or otherwise incorporated as fully as if they were all signed by the Merchant.
One of the Bills of Lading must be surrendered duly endorsed in exchange for the goods of delivery order.

IN WITNESS whereof the Master of the said vessel has signed the above Bills of Lading all of this tenor and date, one of which being accomplished the others will be void.

per pro GEEST INDUSTRIES LTD.
By ....

For the Master

PAYABLE AT BARRY

FOR CONDITIONS OF CARRIAGE SEE OVERLEAF.   Dated at Barry

Bill of lading

on demand, or at a fixed or determinable future time, a sum certain in money, to, or to the order of, a specified person, or to the bearer.'

A bill of exchange might be arranged where the importer requires a longer period of credit before settlement. The exporter draws up a bill on the foreign importer who accepts it and returns it to his creditor. The bill may then either be kept by the exporter until the date of payment, negotiated to a third person, or discounted with a bank.

(c) Documentary credit. An exporter may request an importer to make payment by 'documentary credit' which enables him (the exporter) to obtain payment for the goods before the documents are given to the importer. The importer asks his bank to confirm that settlement will be made when the documents of title are handed over.

(d) Letter of credit. Here the importer's bank guarantees the credit and financial standing of its customer and undertakes to make the payment in due course. The letter of credit is the confirmatory letter from the debtor's bank sent to the importer when the goods are ordered.

(e) Documentary bill. This is a bill of exchange with all documents of title attached, including the invoice and insurance policy which gives the bank the right to take possession of the goods if the bill of exchange is dishonoured at maturity (when it is due).

Questions

1 Explain all the stages and forms used from the time an enquiry is made to a manufacturer up to the time actual payment is made for the goods.
2 Describe the methods of payment commonly used in foreign trade.
3 What is a bill of exchange?
4 Make a list of the types of forms you would require if you were a merchant engaged in both the import and export trade.
5   (i) What is the purpose of a statement?
   (ii) What is the meaning of 'terms of payment'?
   (iii) Explain the meaning of E. & O.E. at the bottom of a statement.

13   Legal aspects of business

Law of contract

The Law of Contract is a very important aspect of business. Thousands of contracts are made each day in the business world and it is therefore necessary that students of business understand the principles of the Law of Contract.

Definition A contract is a legally binding (hence enforceable by law) agreement made between two or more persons, by which rights are acquired by one or more persons to act on the part of the other or others. An examination of the definition would show that for a contract to be enforceable, the agreement must give rise to rights and obligations, *and* the parties concerned must have a distinct intention to create a legal relation between them: i.e. to create legal rights and obligations. Thus a mere agreement between two men is not a contract.

Examples:

 (i) If A promises to take B to work each day on his motor cycle, then breaks the agreement, this is a mere social arrangement and is not enforceable by law.

(ii) If A and B arrange to take equal shares in a pools competition but, on winning the pool, B breaks the arrangement, B could be made to share the pool with A.

A contract may come about when:

 (i) A offers to make a promise, followed merely by B assenting. Such a contract must be under seal.

 (ii) A makes a promise to B, for an act to be performed by B.

(iii) A offers a promise for a promise by B.

For a contract to be valid it must contain the following features:

1   **Offer and acceptance** This may be done orally or in writing, or it may be inferred from the conduct of the parties. It may not be made under seal unless the contract requires a deed.

2   **Form or consideration** For a contract to be valid either form, i.e. the solemn formalities of a contract under seal which compensates

for a lack of consideration, or consideration must be present.

3   **Capacity of the parties** Their status must be such that in the eyes of the law they have power to bind themselves in a contract.

4   **Legality** The subject-matter of the contract must not be contrary to law.

5   **Possibility** Performance of the contract must be possible. However, impossibility does not necessarily void a contract.

6   **Genuineness of the consent of the parties** There must be agreement between parties (consensus) and each party must have entered into the contract of his own free volition (will).

7   **Good faith** There must not be undue influence or duress, mistake, fraud or misrepresentation.

If one or more of these essential features is lacking, the contract will be either void or voidable.

However, it must be noted that a mere declaration of intention to offer is not an offer as there is no intention that such a declaration should be accepted, and so it cannot, therefore, form the basis of a contract.

Following from the above one must make a distinction between an invitation to trade, e.g. advertising the price of a house, and an offer which is capable of acceptance. Also a distinction must be made between a mere statement of an invitation to tender and the tender itself, which is the offer, and which must be accepted for there to be a contract.

OFFER AND ACCEPTANCE
A contract comes into existence when a definite offer has been unconditionally accepted, i.e. when there is agreement of minds between the parties as to the common intention contemplated in the agreement. However, should the acceptance be conditional upon the drawing up of a formal contract, then the contract does not arise until that has been done.

Rules governing offer and acceptance
(a)   (i) An offer must be communicated to the other party.

(ii) The offer may be made generally or to a definite person, but acceptance must be made by a specific person or persons.

(b)   The offerer may attach any conditions he pleases, but these conditions must be brought to the offeree's notice at the time of the offer being made, if the offeree is to be bound by them. Some examples are bus tickets, laundry books, etc. which contain conditions limiting liability for loss or damage.

(c)   The offerer cannot bind the other party to the contract by an attempt to dispense with a communication of acceptance, i.e.

acceptance must be communicated to the offerer. However, performance of the act required in the offer may be considered sufficient communication, as in the case of offer by advertisement. There must be some positive act on the part of the offeree to constitute acceptance.

(d) The offer may be revoked at any time before acceptance unless valuable consideration has been given to keep the offer open for a certain time, e.g. an option is created. If A offers to sell his house to B at a certain price and B replies that he will think it over and let him know during the month, B will have no case if, on deciding to purchase the house within the month, he finds that A has sold it. If, however, B had given $5,000 to A to keep the offer open for one month, B then has an option to purchase, which, within the time period, is an acceptance of A's offer to sell. If A sells the house in the meantime this would be a breach of the option agreement.

(e) Revocation must be communicated to the offeree. To be effective, revocation must actually reach the offeree before he has accepted, otherwise it is inoperative.

(f) Acceptance must be unconditional. An offer must be accepted in all its terms. Any attempt to accept the offer with a modification of the terms is not an acceptance but a refusal and a counter offer, which will itself require acceptance before a contract emerges.

(g) An offer can be accepted only by the party to whom it is made and acceptance must be communicated. The offerer or his agent must be notified unequivocally, by words or conduct, of the acceptance of the offer. Where the offer was made by advertisement, the performance of the conditions outlined in the advertisement amounts to communication of acceptance.

(h) Acceptance must be within the time stipulated or within a reasonable time, and without notice of any revocation of the offer. Acceptance is final and irrevocable, and once made, a complete contract exists.

(i) An offer lapses:
   (i) when the stipulated time has expired, or, if no time has been mentioned, then after the expiry of a reasonable time.
   (ii) when it is rejected by the offeree.
   (iii) on the death of either offerer or offeree before acceptance. However if the offer was accepted and a contract constituted before the death of either party, the contract is still valid, even though some further steps are necessary to give effect to the contract.

114

(j) Use of the post:
  (i) The offer is complete only when it actually reaches the offeree. An offer lost in the post is no offer at all.
  (ii) Acceptance is effected when the letter is actually posted. An acceptance lost in the post and which never reaches the offerer is nevertheless valid, and a contract existed from the time of posting by the offeree.

CONSIDERATION

Consideration may be defined as the price (not necessarily a monetary one) for which one party secures the legal obligation on the part of the other. Consideration may be either 'good' or 'valuable'. 'Good' consideration consists of natural love and affection and is not sufficient to support a simple contract. Consideration sufficient to support a simple contract must be 'valuable' consideration, that is, some right, interest, profit or benefit accruing to one party, or some forebearance, detriment, loss or responsibility given, suffered or undertaken by the other.

Valuable consideration is the price for which one party secures the undertaking on the part of the other, and it is necessary for the validity of simple contracts.

Rules for consideration

1 **Consideration must be real** This means that it must be something which is well defined, and has some ascertainable value. It should also be transferable and should not be something which one party is already bound to do by law.

2 **Consideration must be lawful** A promise given to commit an unlawful act would be void because the consideration on which it is based is illegal.

3 **Consideration must not be past** This means that motives of gratitude for a benefit received in the past will not support a promise not stated in a deed.

There are three exceptions to the above rules: (i) where it can be shown that services were rendered at the request, expressed or implied, of the promisor; (ii) a debt barred by law (Limitation Act) may be revived by a written acknowledgement of the claim so that it will be enforceable, although the consideration is past; (iii) the Bills of Exchange Act provides that consideration for a bill may be constituted by any consideration sufficient to support a simple contract, or by an antecedent debt or liability.

Consideration may be either executed or executory.

Executed consideration may be defined as consideration which is wholly performed on one side, or by one party, immediately the

115

contract is entered into. An example of executed consideration is the purchase of goods in a shop on credit. The shopkeeper has done all that is due from him in handing over the goods.

Executory consideration, on the other hand, is a promise to confer a benefit or to suffer some detriment at some future time. In the above example of the purchase of goods, the consideration due from the customer is executory in that having received the goods he promises to pay at some future date.

Types of contracts

There are three main types of contracts.

1   **A simple contract** Such a contract requires no special form; it may be oral, written or implied by conduct.
2   **Specialty contract** This type includes a lease of land, hire purchase agreements, sale of goods, etc.
3   **A contract of record** A contract of this type would, for example, be the result of judgement in court.

SIMPLE CONTRACTS

As we said above, a simple contract may be (i) in writing; (ii) oral; (iii) implied by conduct.

Simple contracts are the most common form of contract experienced. The average person or businessman makes several every day of his life. e.g. for travel, purchases of personal needs, hailing a taxi, or refreshment. Consideration is a most essential element in simple contracts.

The following simple contracts must be in writing:

(a)   Assignments of copyright;
(b)   Contracts of marine or life insurance;
(c)   Bills of exchange and promissory notes;
(d)   Hire-purchase, credit-sale or conditional sale agreements.

These contracts must be under seal:

(a)   Lease for more than three years;
(b)   Conditional bill of sale;
(c)   Gratuitous promises.

SPECIALTY CONTRACTS (CONTRACTS BY DEED)

These are contracts dealing with mortgages, sale of goods, sale of land, insurance.

An agreement for the sale or lease of land must be made in writing, but the actual conveyance of the land must be by deed, as must also the actual lease if it is for more than three years.

Characteristics of specialty contracts

(a) Both sealing and signature are necessary.
(b) As long as there is an intention to seal no mark or impression is necessary.
(c) Attestation by one or more witnesses is customary but not necessary.
(d) A deed must be delivered by the promisor. Delivery is the act of handing the deed to the other party. This may be either actual or constructive. By constructive we mean the person indicates by certain words, in front of a witness, an intention to deliver, e.g. the person places his finger on a wafer and says: 'I deliver this as my act and deed.'
(e) Delivery may be made subject to a condition to be performed later. Such a deed is termed an 'escrow'.

CONTRACTS OF RECORDS

Such contracts are obligations imposed upon a person by the Court acting in its judicial capacity, e.g. ordering a man to maintain his child. Such contracts are of two kinds:

(a) Judgements of a Court of Record;
(b) Recognisances, by which a person is bound over to be of good behaviour or to keep the peace.

Another type of contract includes those implied by law (quasi-contracts), where the Court implies a fictitious promise to pay on the part of the defendant, although in fact no such promise, and no agreement whatever, has been made.

Discharge of contract

A contract is discharged when the promisor ceases to be bound by its obligations.

METHODS OF DISCHARGE

1 **By performance** Performance means that the contract has been fulfilled in every respect.
2 **By breach** If A promises to do something for B upon the condition that B in turn does something for A, and B breaks his side of the contract by not doing what he promised to do, then A is discharged by breach.
3 **By renunciation** In this case A expressly by implication refuses to perform the contract, or after performing it, refuses to continue further performance.

4   **By impossibility** Where an undertaking is known by both parties to be too absurd to be capable of performance, or where it is obviously impossible, according to present standard of human achievement, no contract can arise. Also a contract to do what is prohibited by law is void.

5   **By agreement** This may be due to: (i) accord and satisfaction; (ii) release, a waiver given for no consideration by one of the parties who perform this part: release must be effected by deed since no consideration is present; (iii) waiver, i.e. the parties mutually waiving their rights before performance by either has taken place; (iv) the substitution of a new agreement for an old.

6   **By lapse of time** An action founded in contract must be brought within a certain period. (Limitation Act).

7   **Merger** The substitution of a higher grade of contract for a lower one.

8   **Bankruptcy** Here the rights and liabilities of a bankrupt rest in the trustee who can perform or enforce contractual obligations and disclaim onerous contracts. Personal service contracts do not pass to the trustee.

9   **Death** Here all rights and liabilities upon contracts pass to the personal representatives, except in the case of contracts for personal services.

Questions

1   Distinguish between offer, acceptance and consideration.
2   (a) What is a simple contract?
     (b) What are the rules governing a simple contract?
3   What are the chief characteristics of specialty contracts?

14   Marketing

What is marketing?

Our whole lives, from dawn to dusk each day, are touched by some aspect of marketing. For example, we sleep in a Slumberfome bed, we have Kellogg's Cornflakes for breakfast, we brush our teeth with Colgate toothpaste, we drive to school in an Austin car, and so on. Thus right through the day we are surrounded and touched by aspects of marketing.

Marketing is not selling or promotion. Selling and promotion are only parts of several marketing functions.

Marketing is human activity, and effort, directed at satisfying needs and wants through the exchange processes.

The most basic concept underlying marketing is that of human needs, which is a state of felt deprivation in a person. Human needs are plentiful and complex, varying from simple physiological needs for food, clothing and shelter to the higher needs of love, affection and self-expression. When needs are not satisfied, people feel deprived and unhappy. An unsatisfied person will (i) look for something that will satisfy the need, or (ii) try to extinguish the need.

The second basic concept in marketing is that of human wants. Wants are the form human needs take as shaped by a person's culture and individuality. Wants are described in terms of culturally defined objects that will satisfy needs.

Wants become demands when backed by purchasing power. For example, we may want a mango, but only when we are prepared to pay the going price for that mango is our want transferred into effective demand. In order to satisfy human needs, wants and demands, products must be available. A product is defined as anything that can be offered to a market for attention, acquisition, use, or consumption that might satisfy a want or need.

Marketing takes place where people decide to satisfy needs and wants through the process of exchange. Exchange is the act of obtaining a desired object from someone in return for something else. For exchange to take place the following conditions must be met.

(a) There must be at least two parties.
(b) Each party has something that may be of value to the other party.
(c) Each party is free to accept or reject the other's delivery.
(d) Each party must be capable of communication and delivery.
(e) Each party believes it is appropriate or desirable to deal with the other party.

The measure of a unit of exchange is a transaction which consists of a trade of values between two parties.

The final concept in relation to marketing is that of markets. A market is the set of actual and potential buyers of a product. Thus, marketing means working within markets to create exchange for the purpose of satisfying human wants and needs.

Some concepts of marketing management

The production concept holds that consumers will favour those products that are available and highly affordable, and therefore management should concentrate on improving production and distribution efficiency.

The product concept holds that consumers will favour those products that offer the best quality, performance and features and provide energy towards making continual product improvements.

The selling concept states that consumers will not buy enough of the firm's products unless the firm undertakes a substantial selling and promotion campaign.

The marketing concept holds that the key to achieving organisational goals consists of determining the needs and wants of target markets and delivering the desired forms of satisfaction more effectively and efficiently than your competitors.

The societal marketing concept holds that the task of the firm is to determine the needs, wants and interests of target markets and to deliver the desired form of satisfaction more effectively and efficiently than competitors in such a way that the consumer's and society's well-being is enhanced and/or preserved.

The functions of marketing

These may be divided into four groups:

(a) to aid and stimulate maximum consumption, which will in turn create maximum production, employment and wealth;
(b) to maximise consumer satisfaction and not just consumption;

(c) to maximise product variety and consumer choice, thus to enable consumers to find those goods that precisely satisfy their tastes, allowing consumers to maximise their life-styles and, therefore, their satisfaction;

(d) to improve the 'quality of life' which consists of
   (i) the quality, quantity, range, accessibility, and cost of goods,
   (ii) the quality of the physical environment, and
   (iii) the quality of the cultural environment.

The marketing environment

The marketing environment consists of the actors (people, firms, etc.) and forces that are outside the firm and that affect the marketing management's ability to develop and maintain successful transactions with its target customers. The marketing environment affects the firm significantly because it is always changing, limiting and uncertain.

A firm's marketing environment may be divided into two sections:

(a) the forces close to the company which affect its ability to serve its customers, for example the firm's suppliers, competitors, marketing intermediaries (middle men) and policies. These forces are called its micro-environment;

(b) the larger societal forces such as the demographic (population), economic, natural, technological, political and cultural forces. These larger forces affect the micro-environment and are referred to as macro-environment.

The marketing mix

The concept of the marketing mix is one of the major concepts in modern marketing. The marketing mix is defined as the set of controllable marketing variables that the firm blends to produce the response it wants in the target market. It consists of everything the firm can do to influence the demand for its product. The possibilities open to the firm are generally grouped into four categories known as the 'Four P's':

1 **Product** or the 'goods and services' combination that the company offers to the target market.

2 **Price** or the amount of money that customers have to pay to obtain the product.

3 **Place** or the various activities that make the product available to target consumers.

4 **Promotion** or the various activities undertaken by the company to communicate the merits of its product and to persuade target customers to buy it.

121

Marketing research

Marketing research may be defined as the systematic gathering, recording and analysing of data about problems relating to a specific marketing situation facing the firm.

The main objective of marketing research is to reduce decision risk by providing management with relevant, timely and accurate information. To understand its customers, competitors, dealers, etc. every firm needs to carry out marketing research. Managers who use marketing research need to know enough about it so that they can get the right information at a reasonable cost.

THE MARKET RESEARCH PROCESS

There are five steps in the marketing research process.

1 **Defining the problem and research objectives** If research finds are to be useful they must be linked to problems facing the company.
2 **Developing information sources** Here the type of information needed and the most efficient ways of collecting this information are determined.
3 **Collecting the information** This may be done by a questionnaire, for example.
4 **Analysing the information collected** Here the data collected are sorted and the relevant data taken out and displayed in tables, graphs, etc.
5 **Presenting the findings** This is the final step. Only major finds that are useful for marketing decisions facing the firm should be presented.

Let us consider more closely step two — information resources. A researcher can gather the following types of information:

(a) **primary data**, which consist of originally collected information for the specific purpose at hand;
(b) **secondary data** consisting of information that already exists somewhere, having been collected for another purpose.

Primary data may be collected in three broad ways:

(a) by observation of people and their setting, for example observing people buying food at supermarkets;
(b) by experiments — selecting matched groups of subjects, giving them different treatment, controlling variables and checking on whether observed differences are significant. The purpose here is to see cause-and-effect relationships by eliminating competing explanations of the observed findings;
(c) by surveys — these are undertaken to learn about people's knowledge, beliefs, preferences, satisfaction levels, etc., and to measure

their strengths in the population. Surveys are best suited for descriptive research.

There are two main methods of collecting primary research data — the questionnaire and mechanical devices. The questionnaire consists of a set of questions presented to respondents for their answers. Usually a sample — a segment of the population selected to represent the population as a whole — is taken when using the survey method.

The following contact methods can be used for getting responses from questionnaires:

(a) telephone interviewing — the best method for getting information quickly;
(b) the mail questionnaire — the best method for reaching persons who will not give personal interviews, or who may be biased by interviewers;
(c) personal interviewing — the most versatile method.

Product and brands

What is a product? Earlier in this chapter we defined a product as anything that can be offered to a market for attention, acquisition, use or consumption that might satisfy a want or need. The term includes physical objects, services, places, organisation and ideas.

A product item is a distinct unit that is distinguishable by size, price, appearance, or some other attribute. For example, soap is a product. A 95c. bar of Refresh is a product item. Products may be classified into three groups according to durability or tangibility.

Durable goods	Non-durable goods	Services
Many-use goods, e.g. clothing, furniture	Consumed in one or a few uses, e.g. beer, soap	Activities, benefits, or satisfaction offered for sale

We can also classify goods in terms of users, e.g. consumer goods and industrial goods.

Consumer goods

(a) **Convenient goods** These are goods that are usually purchased frequently and with the minimum of effort in comparison buying, e.g. soap, newspapers. Convenient goods may be staples (rice), impulse goods (magazines), or emergency goods (lanterns).

(b) **Shopping goods** These are goods that consumers, in the process of purchasing, generally compare on such bases as suitability, quality, price and style, e.g. furniture, used cars, appliances.

(c) **Speciality goods** These are goods with unique qualities and/or brand identification for which a significant group of buyers is generally willing to make a special effort to purchase, e.g. special brands of fancy goods like cars, stereo equipment, men's suits.

(d) **Unsought goods** These are goods that the consumer does not know about or knows about but does not normally think of buying, e.g. smoke detectors, encyclopaedias, gravestones.

Industrial goods

(a) **Material and parts** These are goods that enter completely the manufacturer's product, e.g. raw materials such as cotton, vegetables, lumber, etc.

(b) **Capital items** These are goods that enter the finished product partly, e.g. factories, computers, tools, typewriters, etc.

(c) **Supplies and services** These are items that do not enter the finished goods at all, e.g. lubricants, typing paper, legal services, window cleaning.

PRODUCT LINE

A product line is a group of products that are closely related, either because they function in a similar manner, are sold to the same customer groups, are marketed through the same types of outlets, or fall within a given price range, e.g. Eves or Grace line of products, or Avon line of products. The product mix is the set of all product lines and items that a particular seller offers for sale to buyers. For example, a producer's product mix may consist of household items, jewellery and cosmetics.

PACKAGING

This covers the activities of designing and producing the container or wrapper for a product.

BRANDING

A brand is a name, term, sign, symbol, or design, or a combination of them, which is intended to identify the goods or services of one seller or group of sellers and to differentiate them from those of competitors.

The brand name is that part of a brand which can be vocalised, e.g. Eve, Pony, Avon.

The brand mark is that part of a brand which can be recognised but is not utterable, such as a symbol, design or distinctive colouring or lettering, e.g. the windmill of Windmill products, the horse on Pony products.

The trademark is a brand or a part of a brand that is given legal protection. A trademark protects the seller's exclusive rights to use the brand name and/or brandmark.

Copyright is the exclusive right to reproduce, publish and sell the matter and form of a literary, musical or artistic work.

PRICING THE PRODUCT

In Chapter Eleven we examined how price is determined in different market structures. In this chapter we shall examine some pricing objectives of firms and some actual pricing methods used by firms.

Pricing objectives

For every product the company has to decide what the objectives are for that particular product. The following are some common objectives.

(a) **Survival**   Some companies set survival as their main objective if the market has too many producers, intense competition and changing consumer wants. To keep their plants going and their products selling, companies must set a low price, hoping that consumers will react to it.

(b) **Current profit maximisation**   The aim here is to set a price that will maximise current profits. Companies estimate the demand and costs associated with alternative prices and choose the price that will produce the maximum current profit, cash flow or rate of return on investment.

(c) **Market share leadership**   Some companies want to be the leaders in market share. The belief is that the company with the largest market share will enjoy the lowest costs and greatest long-run profit. To achieve market share leadership they set prices as low as possible.

(d) **Product quality leadership**   The aim of some companies is to have the highest-quality product on the market. The company will charge a high price to cover the high product quality and high cost of research and development.

Pricing methods

Cost-plus pricing   This is the simplest method. It involves adding a standard mark-up to the cost of the product. For example, a retailer pays a manufacturer $20 for a product, he marks it up by 10% and sells it for $22.

Break-even analysis and target profit pricing   Here the firm tries to determine the price that will produce the profit it is seeking. Target pricing uses the concept of a break-even chart that shows the total cost and total revenue expected at different sales-volume levels. Public utilities use this method of pricing.

Perceived-value pricing Companies that use this method, base the price of their product on their perceived value of the product. They see the buyer's perception of value, not the seller's costs, as the key to pricing.

Going-rate pricing In this method, the firm bases its price largely on competitors' prices, with less attention paid to its own costs or to demand.

Scale-bid pricing Competitive-oriented pricing is used when firms bid for jobs. The firm bases its own prices on expectations of how competitors will price rather than on a relation to its own costs or to demand. The firm wants to win the contract, and this requires pricing lower than the other firms. However, the firm cannot set its price below cost or it will hurt itself financially.

Channels of distribution

A distribution channel is an organised network of agencies, institutions and individuals which together performs all the activities required to link producers with users and users with producers to accomplish the marketing task. The distribution channel allows the seller to locate and supply the users of his merchandise, and allows the user to find and obtain the products he desires.

A channel of distribution may be either direct or indirect. If there is an intermediary such as a wholesaler and a retailer, the channel is indirect. If there is no intermediary then the channel is direct. The function of a distribution channel is to move goods from producers to consumers; to overcome major time, place and possession gaps that separate goods and services from those who would use them.

Types of channels

These can be divided into four groups:

(a) a one-level channel: manufacturer to consumer;
(b) a two-level channel: manufacturer to retailer to consumer;
(c) a three-level channel: manufacturer to wholesaler to retailer to consumer;
(d) a four-level channel: manufacturer to wholesaler to jobber to retailer to consumer.

Some local channels

Retail outlets Examples of these are: department stores, supermarkets, discount stores, variety chain stores, mail order firms, automatic vending machines and door-to-door selling.

Wholesale outlets These are represented by merchant wholesalers, brokers, agents, cash-and-carry wholesalers.

Export trade channels   These may be trade missions, export merchants, joint-selling associations, travelling salesmen, foreign agents or representation.

Marketing agencies

Advertising is a very competitive and specialised field in which all campaigns are highly planned and geared to a particular market. The time and method of presentation, and the media to be used are all carefully considered and calculated to ensure successful advertising.

Advertising firms which specialise and are experts in the techniques of advertising are usually employed by firms to carry out their advertising campaign. These agencies usually receive a fee for their services from the firms whose products are being advertised, and a commission from the owners of the media. Advertising agencies do not only benefit firms, but also media owners who would otherwise have to deal with a large number of individual advertisers instead of a few agencies.

Promoting products

Products need to be effectively communicated to the market. The marketing communications mix consists of four major tools:

(a) **advertising**: any paid form of non-personal presentation and promotion of ideas, goods, or services by an identified sponsor;

(b) **sales promotion**: short-term incentives to encourage purchases or sales of a product or service;

(c) **publicity**: non-personal stimulation of demand for a product, service, or business unit by planting commercially significant news about it in a published medium, or obtaining favourable presentation of it on radio, television or stage that is not paid for by the sponsor;

(d) **personal selling**: oral presentation in a conversation with one or more prospective purchasers for the purpose of making sales.

Each promotional tool has its own unique characteristic and costs. Advertising is a highly public mode of communication; it is persuasive; it is expressive and impersonal. Personal selling is personal, it creates a relationship, and it leads to a response. Sales promotion attracts and communicates, creates an incentive to buy and offers an invitation to make the transaction now. Sales promotion objectives are:

(a) encouraging more usage and purchase of larger-size items;

(b) persuading non-users to try the product;

(c) attracting users of competitors' brands;

(d) encouraging retailers to carry new items and higher levels of inventory;

127

(e) off-setting competitive promotions;
(f) building retailers' brand loyalty;
(g) gaining entry into new retail outlets.

Sales promotion tools include samples, coupons, price packs, premiums and trading stamps.

Advertising has three main objectives.

1   Information advertising tells the market about a new product or suggests new uses of an old product; informs the market of a price change; explains how the product works; describes available services; corrects false impressions and builds a company's image.

2   Persuasive advertising builds brand preferences; encourages switching to your brand; changes customers' perception of product attributes; persuades customers to purchase now and to receive a sales call.

3   Reminder advertising reminds consumers that the product may be needed in the near future; reminds them where to buy it; keeps it in their minds during 'off' seasons.

The most common examples of advertising media are newspapers, television, radio, direct mail and magazines.

Publicity is used to promote brands, products, places, ideas, activities and organisations. The tools of publicity are press relations, product publicity, lobbying, counselling and corporate communication.

Questions

1   What do you understand by the term marketing?
2   What is the 'marketing mix'?
3   Why is marketing necessary?
4   Outline the marketing research process.
5   Distinguish between advertising, sales promotion and publicity.
6   If you were going to market vegetables,
    (a) What form of promotion would you use? Why?
    (b) What distribution channels would you use? Why?

15 Transportation

Transportation is that productive service which deals with movement of commodities and people from one geographical location to another. In order for transportation to take place there must be some 'way', e.g. land, water, air; some 'vehicle', e.g. lorry, rail, boat, schooner, aircraft, and some 'motive force', e.g. human power (walking), water or wind power, electricity, etc.

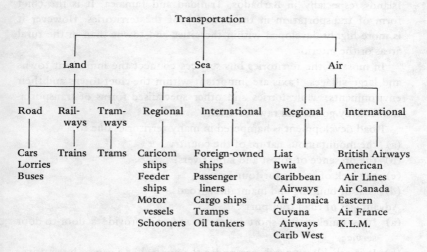

Branches of transportation

Importance of transportation

Transportation is of vital importance to us in the Caribbean. Separated as we are by water, we need transportation to bridge the intervening spaces. We also need a good transportation system to move, quickly and cheaply, food and raw materials within each territory, between territories and to and from foreign countries. Transportation is also very important to our tourist industry. We need fast and cheap transportation to bring the tourists to our shores, to move them from territory to territory and to carry them on tours within each tourist territory. Transportation is also very important to our development. It assists in the opening up of new territories, e.g. the interior of Guyana. It is a means of linking communities, e.g. isolated rural districts and the chief towns, and is vital to our industrialisation drive as workers need adequate transportation, and raw materials and finished goods need to be transported quickly and cheaply.

Transportation by land

Land transportation takes place either by road or rail.

ROAD TRANSPORT
Road transport is fairly well developed in most of the Caribbean Islands, especially in Barbados, Trinidad and Jamaica. It is the chief form of transportation in the majority of the territories. However it is more highly developed within the cities and towns than in the rural areas or the interior.

In most of the territories bus services connect the important towns and large villages. Taxis are important within the chief towns and their environments, while lorries and other specialised forms of transportation convey goods and raw materials.

Road development is hampered in many territories due to:
(a) the mountainous nature of the country;
(b) the presence of forest and large rivers;
(c) the lack of stones for foundations;
(d) cost of building and maintaining roads.

Advantages of road transport
(a) It is quicker for short journeys and can provide a door-to-door service.
(b) It is reliable as goods are under the control of a van or lorry driver until delivered to the buyer.
(c) Road transport is relatively cheap over short distances.
(d) It is relatively safe for goods, with little handling, and so cuts down on pilfering.
(e) It provides the tourist with more opportunity for sight-seeing.

RAIL AND TRAM
Tramways had been established in some of the territories e.g. Barbados

and Trinidad, in the early part of this century; however they no longer exist today.

Railways, like tramways, were common in some territories, e.g. Barbados, Trinidad and Jamaica, in the early part of this century. Today railways can only be found in Jamaica and Guyana, and in both territories they are important to the bauxite industry. The decline in rail transportation was due mainly to the development of roads and to the high cost of maintenance.

Transportation by water

The Caribbean Islands were discovered by the Arawaks and Caribs, using water transportation, and were later rediscovered by European mariners. For centuries water transportation was the chief link between the territories and the outside world.

RIVERS

In Belize and Guyana, rivers form an important means of transportation. Until recently the Belize River, which is navigable by shallow draught vessels to San Ignacio, was the chief waterway and contributed to the site and growth of Belize city. Timber is still floated down the river.

In Guyana all heavy traffic is river-borne. However the presence of rapids limits the distance which can be travelled by river. Small steamers can reach Bartica on the Essequibo, while punts are used to carry timber and small motor boats are used to transport passengers.

SEA TRANSPORT
We can divide sea transport into regional and international.
Regional shipping
At present regional shipping facilities are provided by private individuals (foreign and local) and by the governments of the region. The West Indies Shipping Company (WISCO) operates three ships, one fully containerised and two carrying both containers and 'break-bulk'. The *Caricom Enterprise* is fully containerised and travels monthly to Trinidad, Guyana and Barbados. The *Caricom I,* another monthly voyager, travels to Trinidad, Barbados, Grenada, St. Lucia, Dominica, Montserrat, St. Kitts and Antigua. It carries both containers and break-bulk goods. The *Mor* makes five weekly trips to Jamaica, St. Kitts, Antigua, Montserrat, Dominica, St. Lucia, Barbados, St. Vincent, Grenada, Trinidad and Guyana. This, too, carries both containers and break-bulk. These ships also carry some passengers. A special feature of regional shipping is the presence of large 'feeder vessels' (foreign-owned). These large cargo ships carry cargo to ports such as Trinidad, Barbados and Jamaica.

The cargo is off-loaded and trans-shipped in smaller vessels, e.g. motor vessels and schooners, to the other islands. These motor vessels and schooners are essential to regional shipping and many of the smaller islands depend upon them for the movement of cargo.

Problems facing regional shipping

The major problem facing regional shipping is how to keep down the cost of transportation. At present inflation and the rising price of fuel are forcing privately owned shipping companies to raise the price of their services. However, WISCO has been attempting to keep prices from rising in spite of increasing fuel and handling charges. This is achieved mainly because regional governments subsidise the company.

Extra-regional trade

Shipping between the Caribbean and the outside world is entirely dependent on foreign-owned shipping facilities. The Caribbean imports from extra-regional sources a very large proportion of its food and other consumer goods, machinery, motor cars and raw materials for use in factories. All of these are carried in foreign-owned vessels, so we can see how much we depend on these foreign shipping companies, and also how much our cost of living is affected by freight rates over which we have little or no control. The foreign shipping companies have organised themselves into Shipping Conferences which fix rates that all member lines will charge their customers. Caribbean governments are not consulted when these freight charges are fixed, and they have no effective method of preventing the implementation of these rates. Thus these rates which are constantly rising are reflected in our ever-increasing cost of living.

Types of ships which come to the Caribbean

Tramp steamers These are medium-sized ships between 8,000 and 15,000 tons and are chartered for particular voyages or for a period of time. They carry cargo all around the world, varying their routes to suit their connections. They carry mainly heavy merchandise such as cement and timber.

Passenger liners These are huge passenger liners, commonly called 'tourist boats' in the Caribbean. They are luxury liners, built mainly for the convenience of their passengers. They usually travel along special routes and to an arranged schedule. They may carry some light cargo, some surface mail and parcels.

Cargo liners These are smaller than the passenger liners and cater mainly for the transportation of foodstuffs, vehicles. They generally have a few cabins for passengers. The refrigerated Geest boats (banana boats) come within this category. Again they travel by special schedule.

Containerised ships Containerisation has been a recent development in the transportation of goods. Containers are standardised metal boxes or crates used for the carriage of bulk supplies or machine parts. Containers can fit special lorries and railway wagons, and can also be fitted easily into the holds of ships. They provide protection from damage and pilfering, reduce handling costs and save time. The use of containers also cuts down on insurance charges. Special containerised ships are now carrying cargo stored in a number of containers.

Special purpose ships. These are such ships as oil tankers, ships carrying molasses and chemicals, refrigerated ships and containerised ships.

Advantages of sea transport

(a) The *way* is free and gives access to most parts of the world.

(b) Only a small amount of power is needed to drive a vessel so that economies can be achieved by building large ships.

(c) It is very suitable for heavy goods due to the fact that the buoyancy of the water makes the effective weight zero. This means that ships can be big but strong, e.g. super-tankers.

Transportation by air

Air transport is by far the most important means for the movement of people, both within and from outside the region. Our tourist industry depends heavily upon air transport. The movement of goods by air is becoming increasingly important and steps are being taken to develop a regional cargo carrier for the transportation of goods.

The Caribbean is well served by a number of foreign-owned airlines, e.g. British Airways, American Airlines, Air France, Air Canada, Royal Dutch Airlines. There are also some airlines owned by local governments, e.g. British West Indian Airways which is owned by Trinidad and Tobago, Caribbean Airways which is owned by Barbados, Air Jamaica and Guyana Airways Corporation. These are all international airlines serving foreign as well as regional routes. There are nine international airports within the Caricom region, Timehri in Guyana, Piarco in Trinidad, Grantley Adams in Barbados, Norman Manley and Montego Bay in Jamaica, St. John's in Antigua, Vieux Fort in St. Lucia, Nassau and Freeport in the Bahamas. Apart from these all the other islands have an airport or at least an airstrip.

Regionally, Liat (1974) Limited, a regional airline, serves most of the smaller islands. There are also several small charter services and tours to the islands. Trinidad and her sister island, Tobago, are served by Trinidad Airlines Limited, while Air Guyana serves a number of towns and villages in the interior of Guyana.

The two most important cargo air services are Carib West of Barbados (now being amalgamated with B.W.I.A.) and Guyana Airways.

Advantages of air transport

It is essential to remember that in air transport the actual cost of the air freight ticket is less important than the overall cost of moving goods from their present position to their destination. The overall cost includes many other expenses beside the actual carriage charge.

(a) Compared to those for sea transport, packing costs for air transport are very low. Most aircraft fly above the clouds, high above the sea so that the goods in transit are not affected by weather conditions.

(b) In air transport, factory conditions can be preserved. Special racks installed in the aircraft enable goods to be delivered in perfect condition.

(c) Insurance costs are lower by air. This is because the duration of the journey is generally short, so that for any given transit the risks are much smaller than those incurred by ships.

(d) Use of air transport saves time which may prevent losses by idle factories or over-stocked warehouses.

(e) Use of air transport enables fashionable goods to sell at the crest of the fashion wave.

Factors to consider in choosing the means of transport:

(a) The distance to be travelled.

(b) The nature of the goods to be transported, i.e. size, weight and volume, value.

(c) Perishability, i.e. how long the goods can last, whether they need special refrigeration facilities or special handling.

(d) Urgency i.e. how soon the goods are needed at their destination.

(e) Cost of handling.

Importance of good sea and airport facilities

The transportation of goods is a costly business which can add considerably to the price consumers must pay for commodities.

A good terminal (sea or air) should be one which facilitates the swift distribution of goods at the least cost possible. It should provide facilities for the speedy unloading and safe storage of goods. Also the removal of goods from the terminal should be done with the least hindrance (red tape) possible.

There should be adequate facilities for the servicing of aircraft or ships, e.g. bulk gasoline supplies and fuelling systems, adequate water supplies, electricity, fork-lifts and cranes and a good stevedoring and long-shore service. Harbours should have adequate dock space, while airports should have adequate parking space for aircraft. There should be refrigeration facilities for perishable foods, e.g. meat and vegetables. Warehousing charges should not be too high, and last, but by no means least, the terminal should be within a reasonable distance of the main commercial centre or town.

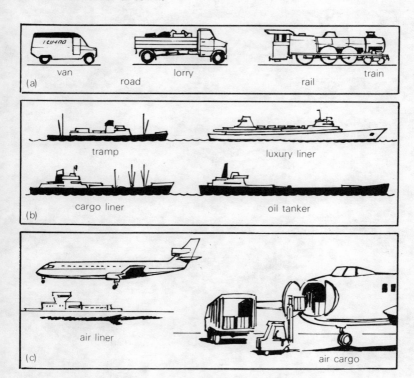

Transportation (a) land (b) sea (c) air

Most ports in the Caribbean are run by some government Port Authority.

Questions

1 What are the functions of your local Port Authority?
2 What are the procedures for docking and warehousing in your country?

3 Of what importance is transportation to the Caribbean?
4 Describe the different forms of transportation in the Caribbean.
5 What are the problems which shippers face in the Caribbean?
6 How important is provision of adequate sea and airport facilities in the Caribbean?

16 Communications

Communications can be defined as a system of facilities used for communication of messages or orders; an organisation that develops, operates and maintains services for communication, e.g. Textel. The word communication simple means 'getting in touch', i.e. sending messages, orders and instructions speedily and accurately.

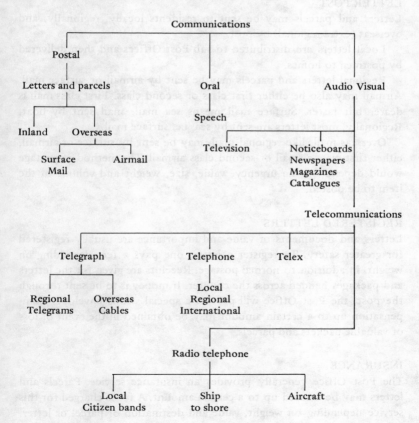

Good means of communication are very important in the world of business. Traders need to keep in touch with each other and with happenings in the market in general. Producers need to be in touch with suppliers of raw materials and with customers. Customers must be informed about new products and price changes. The Post Office, telephone, radio, television, cable and telex are some of the means of communication.

Services provided by the Post Office

The main services provided by Post Offices in the Caribbean are the delivery of letters and parcels, registration of letters, private boxes and Post Office bags, insurance, telegrams and the reply paid service.

LETTER POST
Letters and parcels may be sent to residents locally, regionally, and overseas (extra-regional) by post.

Local letters are distributed to sub Post Offices and then delivered by postmen to homes.

Regional letters and parcels may be sent by airmail or surface mail. Airmail may also be either first class or second class. First class mail is dearer but faster. Surface mail means sea mail: mail sent by boat. Regionally, most letters are sent by sea, i.e. surface mail.

Overseas mail, like regional mail, may be sent by surface or airmail, either first class airmail or second class airmail. The method of postage would depend on the urgency, value, size, weight and volume of the item to be posted.

REGISTERED LETTERS
Letters and documents of value and importance are usually registered for greater safety. To register a letter, one pays a fee, depending on weight, in addition to normal postage. Receipts are given for the letters and packages handed across the counter. If money is to be sent through the post, the Post Office will provide a special strong envelope. Compensation up to a certain amount may be obtained in the event of loss of valuable packets and parcels.

INSURANCE
The Post Office generally provides an insurance service. Parcels and letters may be insured up to a certain amount. A fee is charged for this service depending on weight, value and destination of parcel or letter.

PRIVATE BOXES AND POST OFFICE BAGS

Individuals, organisations and firms can obtain the use of a private Post Office box, or arrange for mail to be collected and delivered to their destination in one batch ahead of the normal delivery time. A small fee is charged for this service.

BUSINESS REPLY SERVICE

West Indian Post Offices offer a limited business reply service. This is done mainly through the use of A.P. cards. These are enclosed in letters from businessmen or firms to clients and prospective customers, to encourage them to reply. The client fills in the information asked for on the card and the postage is paid by the addressee. A fee is charged for this service.

TELEGRAMS

Post Offices also offer a telegram service to customers. The charge is dependent upon the number of words and destination of the telegram.

TELECOMMUNICATIONS

A little over a century ago a practicable way was found to send long-distance messages more rapidly than a man could carry them. This proved to be one of the most important and fundamental changes in the history of mankind. With the invention of the submarine cable, a printed exchange and later a verbal exchange could be made across the globe in a matter of minutes, thus bringing distant places closer. The telecommunication revolution had begun, and in that revolution the Caribbean was not neglected. Within a few years of the laying of the first Atlantic cable, the Caribbean was linked to the global network.

The islands were first linked together in 1871. The first telegraph companies in the Caribbean were:
(a) The West Indies and Panama Telegraph Company (in 1873 this company linked the Caribbean to the global network);
(b) The Western Telegraph Company (in 1920 this company linked the Caribbean and North and South America);
(c) The Pacific Cable Board, which started in 1924 and expanded ship to shore radio operations in the Caribbean.

Later these companies joined to form Cable and Wireless, a company which continues to expand and upgrade the international telecommunication services of the Caribbean. Textel, Trinidad and Tobago External Telecommunications Co. Ltd, is an associate of Cable and Wireless (West Indies) Ltd.

Services offered by Cable and Wireless and Textel

TELEGRAPHY

Telegrams originating in any territory are processed rapidly through a message-switching computer to destinations around the globe, a basic requirement in this world of instantaneous exchange of information in the sphere of business.

TELEX

There is a rapidly growing telex service which is an extension of telegraph communication, offering the additional advantage of a direct person-to-person, office-to-office, service for instantaneous query and reply. Under consideration at present is the establishment of an automatic telex switch making it even easier to establish contact between points. Telex involves the use of a teleprinter, which is a machine like a typewriter, on which messages are typed by the sender. The messages are transmitted to a similar machine which reproduces them on tape or on sheets of paper in the receiving office.

TELEPHONE

The Caribbean is linked to the world by the international automatic telephone service, which permits people to speak on the telephone to friends, relatives and business associates with clarity as good as that normally experienced in person-to-person conversations within each territory.

FACSIMILE TRANSMISSION

This service makes it possible to bring photographs of events immediately as they occur and not only still photographs but moving films, so that events can be viewed while they are actually in progress.

Questions

1   List the different forms of communications found in your country.
2   Why is a good system of communications necessary to (i) your country; (ii) the Caribbean?
3   How does the Post Office assist communications?
4   Distinguish between a telegram, telex and radio telephone.

17 Money

The characteristics of money

Money may be defined as any commodity which is generally acceptable as both a measure of value and a medium of exchange. The commodity may be cowry shells, beads, cigarettes, precious metal or paper. The important thing is that everybody is prepared to accept it.

For a commodity to be a good medium of exchange:
(a) it must be generally acceptable;
(b) it should be relatively scarce, i.e. the quantity should be controllable;
(c) it should be easily divisible into fractional units;
(d) it should be homogeneous in character;
(e) it should be fairly durable;
(f) it should be portable.

LEGAL TENDER

Legal tender is money which the State declares can be used for the payment of debts up to any amount, e.g. bank-notes in the Caribbean. If you examine a bank-note you will find the words 'These notes are legal tender for the payment of any amount' written on it. Coins are limited legal tender in that they are legal tender up to specified amounts.

INTRINSIC VALUE

Money in itself has no value, the paper in a $1 note is worth very little, but by common consent it is accepted as a measure of value which is assumed to be $1. When, however, the commodity money mentioned above was used, the commodities had to be valuable for their own sake, e.g. for use as ornaments.

The early coins were minted with a known weight and fineness of metal, which meant that the value of the coin corresponded to the value of the metal, e.g. a $1.00 gold coin was supposed to have $1's worth of gold metal, and a 2 shilling silver coin had 2 shillings' worth of silver. These coins had an intrinsic value which caused some people to melt them down to make ornaments. Today the metal content of coins is no longer worth as much as the face value of the coins.

THE FUNCTIONS OF MONEY

1 **Money is a medium of exchange** This is the main function of money. It gives the consumer a freedom of choice which he would not possess under barter.
2 **Unit of account** It provides a means by which goods and services can be given a price. It is also used for economic calculations.
3 **A store of value** Money can be stored for future spending. However, this function of money can be satisfied only if (i) it retains its value; (ii) goods and services are available when required.
4 **A means of deferred payments** Money makes possible credit transactions. Because of this function business capital can be borrowed to finance production; consumers can buy goods on hire purchase or some other form of credit.
5 **The price mechanism** Money makes possible the working of the price mechanism, i.e. money registers demand and assigns prices to goods and services.

THE VALUE OF MONEY

When looking at money as a store of value we said that this function can only be satisfied if money retains its value. What then is the value of money? We all know that when prices are high, a given unit of money can purchase fewer goods than when prices are low. The value of money then is related to its purchasing power, i.e. how much a given unit of money would buy. When prices are rising the value of money falls, and when prices are falling the value of money increases.

THE IMPORTANCE OF MONEY

(a) Money makes production possible in a modern complex economic system.
(b) Money simplifies both the process of production and distribution of goods and services, if for their productive services people are paid money wages.
(c) Money makes specialisation, division of labour and modern large scale production possible.
(d) Money makes saving possible. Saving is necessary if investment is to take place.
(e) Money makes a credit system including the price of borrowing (interest rates), possible.
(f) Money enables economic growth to occur.

TYPES OF MONEY

1 **Coins** These are 'token money' and are legal tender only up to a small amount.

2 **Bank-notes or paper money** These are issued by the Central Bank in specific denominations, e.g. $1.00; $5.00; $20.00; $100.00. Paper money is really 'faith money' or substitute money, in that it is no longer convertible into gold, and its acceptability depends on the good faith and financial integrity of the government issuing it. Paper money maintains its value in the outside world if the issuing country is able to produce and export sufficient goods to be able to pay for the value of all imported goods. (This point relates to the currency as a whole and not just paper money.)

3 **Bank deposits** The holder of a bank deposit is allowed to draw cheques on his bank account. A cheque is a written order by the drawer to a banker to pay a specified sum to some person. Cheques are not legal tender and it is the bank deposit and not the cheque which is considered as money. Cheques are however a convenient and safe method of making payments and are generally acceptable. They are the commonest form of payment used in business today, in so far as they are involved in the greatest value of transactions, although not necessarily in the greatest number.

NEAR MONEY

This includes Postal Orders, Treasury Bills and other Government Securities and Bills of Exchange. They are considered as money by some economists as they can easily be converted into money at short notice.

Money (brief historical perspective)

At the beginning of this century, the principal medium of exchange in the West Indies was United Kingdom coins. Before this a variety of coins were used including Pieces of Eight and Spanish Doubloons. There were two major drawbacks to the use of United Kingdom coins. In the first place there was an absence of satisfactory arrangements for redeeming redundant coins and secondly the United Kingdom retained the seignorage (profit) on the coins issued in the colonies. The West Indian colonies were buying large quantities of coins from the United Kingdom at a price much above their intrinsic value, and had no assurance of getting their money back if they wanted to.

As a result of legislation passed in the United Kingdom authorising

Colonial Governments to issue currency notes in 1902, Trinidad did so in 1906 and by 1941, after many experiments with currency issues, Barbados, Guyana, Trinidad and Tobago agreed to establish a Currency Board.

In May 1946, a West Indian Currency Conference was held in Barbados. This conference recommended the establishment of a Regional Currency Board and the unification of the currency of the eastern group of the West Indies on the basis of the British West Indian dollar worth four shillings and two pence sterling. The result of this recommendation was the establishment of the British Caribbean Currency Board which was given the sole right to issue currency in Barbados, Guyana, the Leeward Islands and Windward Islands and Trinidad and Tobago. The first set of notes was issued on 1st August 1951 and British Caribbean coins on 15th November 1955. The Currency Board system was introduced with three major aims in mind:

(a) to prevent the redundancy of British coins in the territories;
(b) to obtain for the local territories the seignorage of the currency they used;
(c) to maintain the existing convertibility of local currencies.

In effect the board was functioning as a money-changer, issuing physical currency on demand in exchange for bank payments made in sterling for immediate delivery in London. It had no discretionary power as regards issuing, redeeming, managing of portfolio (all reserves were kept in sterling) and investment of reserve funds.

The Currency Board remained in existence until after Trinidad and Tobago and Guyana obtained their independence. Soon after independence these two countries elected to withdraw from participation in the Board, and established their own Central Banks.

With the withdrawal of Trinidad and Guyana, the East Caribbean Currency Authority was established consisting of Barbados, the Windward and Leeward Islands. The objectives of the ECCA were:

(a) to establish a common currency;
(b) to establish an authority to issue and manage the common currency;
(c) to safeguard its international value and to promote monetary stability and a sound financial structure in the territories of the participating governments.

ECCA was to function as a Central Bank. Barbados withdrew from ECCA in 1968 after establishing its own Central Bank. There is now one currency board and several central banks, each issuing its own currency in the Caribbean. This situation will continue until there is a successful effort at political unity in the region.

Questions

1 What are the functions of money? Do notes and coins fulfil these functions?
2 Distinguish between legal tender and money.
3 What do you understand by the term 'near money'?
4 Why is money so important to our economy?

18   Commercial banking

In the last chapter, we examined the role of money in the economy. We must now look at commercial banks which are the institutions which deal mainly with money and which are responsible for releasing money to the public.

A commercial bank is a financial institution which provides money transmission services to its customers. By money transmission services we mean all the services which have to do with the transfer of money from one person or company to another person or company. Such services are honouring of cheques, debit transfer, credit transfer and standing order payments, which will be discussed below.

A commercial bank is a joint stock company owned by its shareholders and controlled by a board of directors. Like any other company it is in business to earn a profit for its shareholders.

Structure of banks in the Caribbean

It must be remembered that most of the banks in the Caribbean are really 'branch banks' with head offices in the United Kingdom, Canada or the U.S. Therefore, most of the top management positions and the decision making functions are located outside the region. Many of the branches however, have a Caribbean head office in one of the larger islands, e.g. Jamaica or Barbados. The Caribbean head offices have a structure similar to that in the figure on page 126.

Functions and services of banks

Commercial banks have three basic functions: accepting deposits, lending funds from the deposits collected, and making payments on behalf of customers.

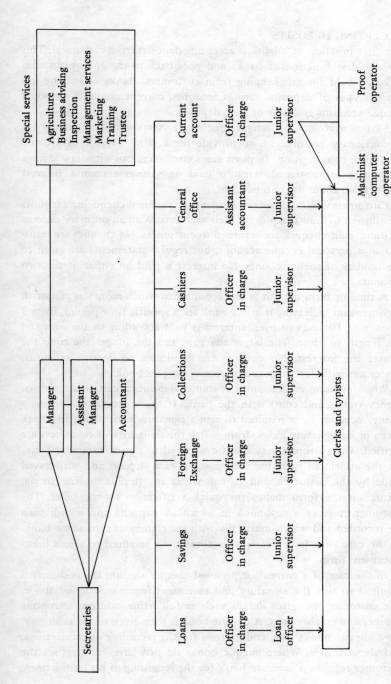

Organisation chart of a bank in the Caribbean

147

ACCEPTING DEPOSITS

The first function of a bank is accepting deposits from customers. This is the oldest function of banks and goes back to the goldsmiths who accepted gold for safe-keeping from customers. Banks accept the following types of deposits: savings accounts, current accounts, personal cheque accounts and time or term deposits.

Savings accounts are designed for small savers who save mainly for precautionary reasons, i.e. to provide for a rainy day, or to provide for future consumption. In most cases customers can withdraw savings without giving notice. Interest is paid on savings accounts. Interest ranges from about 4½ to 6 per cent.

Customers who hold current accounts or personal chequeing accounts are allowed to draw cheques on their accounts. With an ordinary current account, paid cheques are returned to customers. No cheques are returned in a personal cheque account, but regular statements are given to the holders of such accounts. No interest is paid on either of the two accounts.

A time or term deposit is an account into which money is paid with the intention of leaving it in the bank for a specific time period, from 3 months to 10 years or over. Interest is paid according to the sum and the length of time. The larger the sum and the longer the time the greater the interest. No cheques can be drawn on deposit accounts. Customers with deposit accounts receive no pass book.

When opening an account a customer deposits a certain amount of money (notes and coin) with the bank. If the customer is opening a savings account he is required to sign a signature card which the bank keeps in its signature index, from which the signatures of customers are verified. The customer may also be required to sign a statement form. On the statement form the bank records each deposit and withdrawal made by the customer, and his balance at any time is shown. His signature on the form makes for quick verification by the teller. The customer receives a pass-book in which all deposits and withdrawals are recorded and which must tally with the statement card at the bank. In the case of a joint account customers are required to sign a joint-agreement form.

In the case of a current or personal cheque account the customer is required to sign the signature and statement forms mentioned above. The customer also gives details such as full name, address, telephone number and employment. A cheque book is then given to the customer. Most cheque books have counterfoils for the recording of transactions, and deposit slips. Where cheque books do not have counterfoils the customer receives a separate book for the recording of his transactions.

LENDING TO CUSTOMERS

Banks lend money in several ways.

(a) By overdraft: the bank will permit a client to draw cheques for a period, up to a maximum agreed sum over and above the amount of money standing to his credit in his account. Interest is paid only on the actual amount overdrawn. Some current account holders are allowed to be overdrawn up to a fixed sum.

(b) By the loan of a fixed sum for a definite period, at a fixed rate of interest, plus other loan charges. Interest is payable on the entire sum and is calculated when the loan is made.

(c) By financing hire-purchase transactions (ready credit). This is done by channelling funds into finance companies and other businesses.

(d) By discounting bills of exchange for customers. This enables a customer to postpone payment and his creditor to be paid in full promptly.

(e) By providing business and agricultural loans to small businesses and farmers who need capital for investment or expansion.

(f) By holding Treasury Bills, the bank lends money to Government.

MAKING PAYMENTS ON BEHALF OF CUSTOMERS

(a) Banks will arrange for the transfer of money on behalf of clients, e.g. credit and debit transfer, bank draft.

(b) They can act as agents of payments. A customer may give his bank a standing order to transfer automatically sums needed to make periodic payments on his behalf, e.g. insurance premiums, club fees.

(c) They carry out credit transfers. A credit transfer is simply a transfer of money from the bank account of the debtor to the bank account of the creditor. It is merely a book entry recording the transfer from one account to the other.

(d) They carry out debit transfers. In this case the customer's account is debited on instructions received from, say, an insurance company or tax office without reference to the customer.

(e) A customer may request his bank to pay wages on his behalf. He submits a list of the persons to be paid and details of their banks. His (the customer's) bank will arrange for a direct transfer of the sum due to the accounts of the recipients.

Cheques

The essential points of a cheque are:

(a) The date. The cheque is dated on the day on which it is drawn.

(b) The payee's name. This is the name of the person to whom the cheque must be paid. It is written immediately following the words 'Pay to the order of'.

(b) (i)

CARIBBEAN BANK LTD DATE			Notes	
		CODE NO.	$1	
			$2	
	TO	BANK	$5	
			$20	
		BRANCH	$100	
Cashiers Stamp			TOTAL CASH	
		ACCOUNT	Cheques $	
Paid in by • • • • • • • • • • • • • • • •				

(b) (ii)

CARIBBEAN BANK LTD	DATE OF PAYMENT _____
BRANCH •	

ACCOUNT TO BE CREDITED	AMOUNT

By order of •   Reference No. • • • • •

FINAL PAYMENT OF $ • • • • •   <u>TO BE MADE ON</u> • • • • • • • • •

Other instructions   Debit to • • • • • • • •   Account

Please make the above payments commencing • • • • • • • • • • • • • • • •

and periodically until further notice from me/us in writing
until the date shown above

ADDRESS • • • • • • • • • • • • • • • •   SIGNATURE(S) • • • • • • •

• • • • • • • • • • • • • • • • • •   • • • • • •

• • • • • • • • • •

DATE • • • • • • •   ACCOUNT NO. _____

Functions of a bank
(a) (i) accepting deposits (ii) giving loans
(b) Making easy the transfer of money (i) credit transfer (ii) standing order

```
┌─────────────────────────────────────────────────────────┐
│  B24866                    CARIBBEAN BANK                 │
│                       BRIDGETOWN BARBADOS  _____ 19 __  │
│                                                           │
│  PAY TO THE ORDER OF _____  $ _____ │
│                                                           │
│  _____  DOLLARS    │
│                                                           │
│  PERSONAL CHEQUE ACCOUNT                                  │
│            0299253                _____  │
└─────────────────────────────────────────────────────────┘
```

A cheque

(c) The amount. The amount must be written in words and in figures.

(d) The signature. The person drawing the cheque must sign the cheque at the bottom right-hand corner. His signature must be the same as the specimen signature held at the bank.

(e) Personal cheque account number. On personal cheque account cheques, the account number must be written on the bottom left-hand corner.

(f) Other data. Some cheques possess a branch number, at the top right-hand corner, and sorting data along the bottom edge. Where a counterfoil is attached to a cheque, the customer may record details of the cheque drawn, for checking with his bank statement.

Types of cheques

There are, basically, two types of cheque:

1 **Bearer cheques** These are worded 'Pay . . . . . or Bearer', and would be paid to the person presenting the cheque. These are not very safe cheques.

2 **Order cheques** These are worded 'Pay to the order of', or 'Pay . . . or Order' and would only be paid to the order of the person named after the word 'pay'.

All cheques must be endorsed by the person presenting them for payment. Endorsement means signing the payee's name at the back of the cheque. Cheques can either be open or crossed.

An open cheque is one without crossing, which can be cashed across the counter at the bank on which it is drawn. Such a cheque could possibly be cashed by the wrong person.

A **crossed cheque** (see diagram) has two parallel transverse lines drawn across the face of the cheque. Sometimes the words 'and Co.' are written between the lines. The effect of crossing is to prevent the cheque being paid over the counter. A crossed cheque can only be paid into a bank account. Crossing also provides a means of tracing a cheque, since the holder must use a banking account in order to obtain cash.

The crossing of a cheque can either be:

(a) General, with two parallel transverse lines with or without the words '& Co.' or 'not negotiable'. Such cheques can be passed through any bank.

| B24866 | CARIBBEAN BANK |
| | BRIDGETOWN BARBADOS *7th May* 19 *79* |
| PAY TO THE ORDER OF *John Smith* $ *100* |
| *One Hundred* ——— DOLLARS |
| PERSONAL CHEQUE ACCOUNT *Tom Jones* |
| 0299253 |

General crossing

| B24866 | CARIBBEAN BANK |
| | BRIDGETOWN BARBADOS *7th May* 19 *79* |
| PAY TO THE ORDER OF *John Smith* $ *100* |
| *One Hundred* ——— DOLLARS |
| PERSONAL CHEQUE ACCOUNT *Tom Jones* |
| 0299253 |

Special crossing

(b) Special, with the name of the banker written across the face of the cheque, with or without the parallel lines and the words 'not negotiable'. Such cheques must be paid into the bank named on the face.

Advantages of cheques
(a) They may be made out for any sum of money.
(b) They are of great convenience in remitting money.
(c) They may be made payable to one person only, at one bank.
(d) They are the safest method of transmitting money.
(e) They may be easily traced.
(f) Payment may be stopped by the drawer, if necessary.
(g) They form a record of payments and receipts.
(h) They economise on the use of notes and coins.

OTHER SERVICES
(a) Providing night-safe deposit facilities, thus allowing customers, in particular retailers, to deposit their day's takings safely after the bank is closed.
(b) Issuing letters of introduction, credit information and credit references on behalf of clients.
(c) Providing foreign exchange services for importers and exporters and other customers, also travellers' cheques.

The early banks in the Caribbean

(a) The Colonial Bank which later became Barclays Bank D.C.O., now Barclays International, is the oldest bank in the Caribbean. The first offices of this bank were established in 1837 in Barbados, Jamaica, Guyana, Trinidad and Tobago, Antigua, Dominica, Grenada, St. Lucia, St. Vincent and St. Kitts.
(b) The Colonial Bank was followed by the Bank of Nova Scotia which established its first office in Kingston, Jamaica, in 1889. Nova Scotia was followed by The Royal Bank of Canada which established its first office in Puerto Rico in 1907 and in the Bahamas in 1908. It was not until 1920 that the Canadian Imperial Bank of Commerce, then the Canadian Bank of Commerce, entered the Caribbean with offices in Havana, Kingston and Bridgetown. Apart from these foreign banks, a number of small cooperative 'penny' banks were established in some of the islands by local entrepreneurs. Some, in Grenada and Dominica, are still functioning.

Off-shore banking

One of the latest developments in the field of banking in the Caribbean is the setting up of off-shore banks in a number of territories, e.g. Bahamas, Turks & Caicos Islands and Barbados.

Off-shore banking is the business of:

(a) receiving foreign funds through the acceptance of foreign money deposits payable either on demand or after a fixed period, or the sale or placement of foreign bonds, certificates and other foreign securities;

(b) using the above funds for lending, e.g. loans, advances and investment, and for the use of persons carrying on business;

(c) acceptance in trust of foreign currencies and securities, foreign personal and/or movable properties and real or immovable property.

The benefits of off-shore banking to a country are:

(a) increased employment of clerical and technical personnel;

(b) development of local financial expertise and the training of locals for the top managerial positions in banking institutions;

(c) increase in the number of foreigners visiting the country, as foreign asset-holders will visit the country to see first-hand how their business is being handled;

(d) increase in revenue to the country from licences, fees and taxation on profits and gains.

Questions

1 Make a list of banks in your country under the headings (i) locally owned; (ii) foreign owned.

2 How do commercial banks benefit (i) businessmen, (ii) private individuals?

3 Distinguish between (i) deposit accounts and current accounts, (ii) overdrafts and personal loans.

4 What is a cheque? What advantage does a cheque have over notes and coins?

19 Central banks and development banks

Central banking

In Chapter 17 we looked briefly at the development of money and central banking in the Caribbean from the Monetary Authority to the starting of central banks. At present there are four Central Banks, those of Jamaica, Trinidad and Tobago, Guyana and Barbados, and one Monetary Authority, the ECMA, in the Caribbean.

Why do we need central banks?

THE TRADITIONAL FUNCTIONS OF CENTRAL BANKS

Traditionally, the functions of central banks have been:

(a) the issuing of currency and the regulating of the same;

(b) acting as the government's bank, having responsibility for all government's accounts, lending to the government, supervising government borrowing both local (e.g. issuing of Treasury Bills and other securities), and foreign (e.g. borrowing from International Banks);

(c) being responsible for the country's foreign reserves, e.g. administering foreign exchange controls;

(d) being the government's financial agent, e.g. participating in the meetings of international monetary organisations;

(e) responsibility for monitoring, forecasting and carrying out the government's monetary and economic policies;

(f) being the banker's bank, e.g. acting as a clearing house for banks; issuing notes and coins to commercial banks, holding commercial bank's reserves;

(g) to preserve economic stability;

(h) to inspire local and foreign confidence in the currency;

(i) to supervise the operations of commercial banks.

All the above functions are indeed carried out by central banks in the Caribbean. There are however, three functions which are relevant to developing countries such as ours, which must be added to the traditional functions. These are:

(j) to increase home savings and harness them to development purposes;

(k) to assist in the establishment of financial markets, e.g. a Stock Exchange;

(l) to provide credit for private enterprise, e.g. credit for large-scale industries, credit for agriculture and credit for small businesses.

The questions we must now ask are, 'How do central banks control the economy?' and 'What are the measures at their disposal for carrying out their functions?' There are a number of economic and legal measures which central banks use to control the economy. In fact, there are seven such methods of monetary control in the laws of central banks.

Open-market operations

By open-market operations we mean that the central bank starts buying and selling government securities, e.g. Treasury Bills. All commercial banks have deposits with the central bank, which they treat as equivalent to cash. Therefore, if the central bank sells securities, the buyers will pay for them by cheques drawn on their commercial banks, the amount of which will be deducted from their deposits with the central bank. This would mean a reduction in commercial banks' cash holdings. Now all banks maintain what is called a cash ratio: i.e. they hold a certain percentage of cash in relation to their total deposits. Thus, if their cash holdings are reduced they will be compelled to lower the total of their deposits by calling in loans or by not renewing loans when they fall due. In this way the spending power of borrowers from the banks will be reduced which will be expected to have a disinflationary effect. A purchase of securities by central banks will have the opposite effect. Commercial banks' deposits with the central bank will increase, the cash to deposit ratio will rise and the banks will be able to expand credit. In the Caribbean this method is not very effective as there is no broad and active market for securities.

Variations in central bank reserve holdings, including special deposits

There is a legal reserves requirement to which all commercial banks must adhere. The commercial banks must deposit with the central bank, as a reserve, a percentage of their total deposits. This is considered by banks as part of their liquid assets ratio. (Liquid assets are those assets of a bank which can be easily converted into cash.) Thus, if the central bank increases the legal reserves requirement, commercial banks would have to deposit a greater amount of money with the central bank. This would affect their liquid assets ratio, forcing them to curtail credit.

The central bank can force banks to deposit with it a given percentage of their total net deposits. These special deposits do not count as part of their liquid assets, though they can earn interest. Special deposits can be so high as to affect banks' liquidity ratio, thus forcing the banks to reduce advances to customers.

Variations in the liquid assets ratio

The central bank has the power to dictate to the commercial banks the minimum liquidity ratio which they shall maintain. This liquidity requirement is expressed as a liquid asset ratio showing the ratio of liquid assets (cash in hand or at the central bank, money at call and short notice, bills discounted, other commercial bills) to total assets or deposits. Variation in this liquidity ratio would have an immediate effect upon the commercial banks' ability to extend credit.

Variations in the local assets

The central bank can decide the amount of local assets, e.g. Treasury Bills, other government securities or currency which the commercial banks must hold as part of their total assets.

Changes in the discount/rediscount rate

This is the rate at which the bank is prepared to discount/rediscount bills of exchange. It generally determines the official short-term rate of interest. Thus, use of this measure can make credit more or less expensive according to whether it is high or low, and so control the volume and level of credit.

Selective controls

Of these the most effective controls are those which can be directed in a discriminatory manner to the credit granted by the banks: e.g. hire-purchase restrictions, laws restricting consumer credit for consumer durables and luxury goods.

Moral persuasion

This power is frequently used in the Caribbean and it is assumed to be based on moral considerations and respect for the central bank. It is however really based on the power relations between the two sectors of the banking system.

Development banking

A development bank is a special financial institution, with emphasis on the provision of industrial finance, to aid economic development. Development banks were first established in some of the countries of Western Europe as part of their general effort to catch up on the industrial lead of the United Kingdom. The need for such institutions still exists today in many parts of the world, especially in the developing countries where there is a shortage of finance in both large and small scale enterprises, for long-term as well as for short-term periods, and in all sectors of the economy, industry, agriculture, and government.

157

THE CARIBBEAN DEVELOPMENT BANK

The Caribbean Development Bank was established by an agreement which was signed on October 18, 1969, at Kingston, Jamaica and which came into force on January 26, 1970, for the purpose of 'contributing to the harmonious economic growth and development of the member countries in the Caribbean and promoting economic cooperation and integration among them, having special and urgent regard to the needs of the less developed members of the region.'

Location of headquarters

The permanent headquarters of the Caribbean Development Bank is located at Wildey, St. Michael, Barbados. The building was erected by the Government of Barbados as part of its obligations under the Headquarters Agreement between the Bank and that Government.

Functions

The Bank has the following functions:

(a) to assist regional members in the coordination of their development programmes with a view to achieving better utilisation of their resources, making their economies more complementary and promoting the orderly expansion of their international trade, in particular, intra-regional trade;

(b) to mobilise within and outside the region additional financial resources for the development of the region;

(c) to finance projects and programmes contributing to the development of the region or any of the regional members;

(d) to provide appropriate technical assistance to its regional members, particularly by undertaking or commissioning pre-investment surveys and by assisting in identification and preparation of project proposals;

(e) to promote private and public investment in development projects by, among other means, aiding financial institutions in the region and supporting the establishment of consortia;

(f) to cooperate and assist in the regional efforts designed to promote regional and locally controlled financial institutions and a regional market for credit and savings;

(g) to stimulate and encourage the development of capital markets within the region;

(h) to undertake or promote such other activities as may advance its purpose.

Membership

Membership of the Bank is open to:

(a) States and Territories of the region;

(b) non-regional States which are members of the United Nations or

158

any of its specialised agencies or of the International Atomic Energy Agency.

Admission to membership in the bank may be obtained upon the affirmative vote of two-thirds of the total number of governors representing not less than three-fourths of the total voting power of the members.

The membership of the Bank is now twenty: eighteen regional and two non-regional members. Venezuela and Colombia were admitted to membership as regional members on April 25, 1973 and November 22, 1974 respectively.

Financial resources

The financial resources of the Bank consist of (i) Ordinary Capital Resources comprising mainly subscribed capital and borrowings and (ii) Special Funds Resources which may be established or accepted by the Bank.

Lending activities

The Bank's lending activities are divided into two major categories: ordinary operations and special operations.

Ordinary operations are those financed from the Ordinary Capital Resources of the Bank.

Special operations are those financed from the Special Fund Resources of the Bank.

A project may combine aspects financed by ordinary operations and other aspects financed by special operations.

The Bank may make or participate in direct loans to governments of its regional member countries, to any of their agencies or political sub-divisions and to both public and private entities and enterprises operating within such countries, as well as to international or regional agencies or entities concerned with economic development of the region.

The Bank will not, however, finance an undertaking in the territory of a member if that member objects to such financing.

The Bank's operations provide principally for the financing of specific projects, in such fields as agriculture, livestock, fisheries, forestry, marketing, manufacture, mining, tourism (particularly small and medium sized regionally owned hotels), transportation, housing (low and lower/middle income), student loans, and infrastructure and services related to the development of these sectors of the economy. High priority is given to the financing of regional projects.

Specific private development projects, whose individual financing requirements are not, in the opinion of the Bank, large enough to warrant the direct supervision of the Bank, may be financed through loans or guarantees of loans to national development banks or other suitable entities.

The Bank may also make or participate in loans to facilitate pre-investment and feasibility studies and project preparation if it considers the project to be worthy of detailed investigation.

Article 1 of the Charter requires the Bank to have 'Special and urgent regard to the needs of the less developed members of the region'. Accordingly, while the Bank's ordinary operations embrace all its regional member countries, the major part of its special operations continue to be in the less developed member countries.

Methods of loan financing

In making direct loans or participating in them the Bank, in accordance with Article 15 (n) of the Charter, provides financing by furnishing the borrower with currencies to meet the foreign exchange costs of the project. In exceptional circumstances and to a limited extent, it will provide some local currency to meet local expenditures from the local currency provided by the government of that territory.

However, in practice, because of the impracticability of distinguishing between local and foreign exchange expenditures, and having regard to the economic circumstances of borrowing regional member countries, the borrower is asked simply to make an appropriate contribution to the cost of the project financed by the bank.

NATIONAL BANKS: BARBADOS AS A CASE STUDY

The development of National Banks is a relatively new experience to the Caribbean. Indeed, only a few territories have such a bank, e.g. Barbados and Guyana.

The Barbados National Bank is a unique institution in the Caribbean, and, to some extent, in the Developing World. The Bank has integrated the functions of former public financial institutions such as the Barbados Savings Bank, The Sugar Industry Agricultural Bank, The Agricultural Credit Bank and The Public Officers' Housing Loan Fund. It is also the major shareholder in the Barbados Mortgage Finance Company.

The Barbados National Bank raises funds not only through deposits from householders and firms, but it also engages in long term domestic borrowing through the issue of bonds as well as through external borrowings from international and regional financial institutions. The Bank acts as an agency for developing the saving habit of the people of the country and channelling these savings into productive activities. Much emphasis is placed on the provision of investment loans to socio-economic groups which have been neglected by the traditional banks.

160

Divisions of the Bank and their functions

Agricultural division

The agricultural division of the Bank is responsible for carrying out the following objectives:

(a) ensuring that the agricultural sector of the country has adequate finance for its operations;
(b) giving financial and technical advice and marketing information to farmers;
(c) giving encouragement to the agricultural diversification programme of government through financing selected projects;
(d) promoting private ownership of fishing vessels.

Applications for loans in this division must satisfy the criteria of technological, economic and financial feasibilities. The applicant for a loan must prove satisfactorily that he is engaged in agriculture, fisheries, or agro-industries, that he has a stake in the project, and that he can repay the loan. Loan repayment generally begins after a grace period.

The commercial division

This division offers a comprehensive range of commercial banking services which includes the provision of short term loans, foreign exchange services, discounting of bills, and the accepting of deposits. Customers benefit from lower interest rates on loans, higher rates on savings and fixed deposits, and tax free interest up to $600. A customer can also draw cheques on his Savings Account. The commercial bank also grants loans to business concerns based on the financial competence of the borrower, the market for the product which he is producing and the applicant's credit rating. Applications for such loans must be accompanied by information of part performance of the enterprise as well as projections of its operations.

Mortgage finance division

The function of this division is to finance the building and purchase of houses for the middle and lower income groups in the society. It is hoped that in the future funds would be available to finance mortgages on chattel houses.

Ability to pay is the main criterion in processing of mortgages; customers may be granted up to ninety per cent of the cost of the project. Interest rates are lower than those offered by other lending institutions, and a customer has up to twenty-five years to repay the loan.

Loans are supervised to ensure proper application of funds.

Structure

The Bank is managed by a Board of Governors comprising twelve members appointed by the Minister of Finance. The President of the Bank is Chairman of the board and Vice-President is the deputy Chairman.

Under the President who is the Chief Executive Officer, comes the Chief Finance Officer who is an Executive Director of the Bank as well as Financial Controller of the institution. Next comes the Bank Secretary. He is director general of administrative matters and personnel, and industrial relations. Then comes the Chief Research Officer whose function is to provide a comprehensive research and intelligence service to the President and the Heads of all divisions. The Chief Internal Auditor undertakes the responsibility for the administration of all aspects of Internal Audit activities through the use of reviews, test checks, sampling and conformity to manuals prescribing the operations of the various divisions of the Bank. The Heads of Divisions are responsible for the day-to-day running of each division.

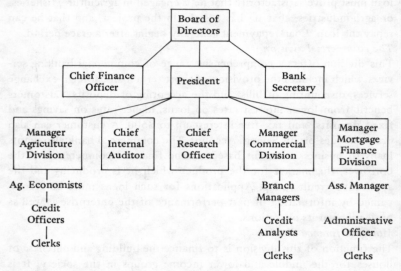

Organisational structure of a national bank

Questions

1 What are the functions of a central bank in the Caribbean?
2 How does a central bank in the Caribbean control the level and volume of credit in the economy?
3 Is the Caribbean Development Bank a central bank? If not, how does it differ from a central bank?
4 How does the Barbados National Bank differ from an ordinary commercial bank?

20 Money and capital markets

In the last three chapters we have been looking at money and banking institutions. In this chapter we shall examine some other financial institutions and their importance to the economy. Before doing this, however, we shall examine the management of money by householders.

Money management and personal budgeting

Wise management of money is necessary if householders are to gain the greatest satisfaction from their money incomes. Everyone who wishes to manage his money to the best advantage should start by making a financial plan.

A BUDGET

A budget is a short-run financial plan. It is a means of carrying out the larger and general financial plan you have made, and helps you use your money just as you wish, making sure that it goes where you want it to. A budget tells you what you can afford and what you cannot; you can decide which uses of your money will give you the most satisfaction.

Included in the financial plan and budget should be some provision for saving. Saving does not mean piling up money for its own sake, but putting money aside for specific purposes. People generally save (i) for emergencies, e.g. loss of job, illness; (ii) to buy something they want in the future, e.g. a home; (iii) to provide for the future, e.g. old age. The amount to be saved will depend on the reason for saving. Savings should appear as a separate item on the budget and a definite sum should be aimed at each week or month, and the sum thus saved should be deposited in a savings account where interest will be received.

Apart from through commercial banks, cooperative banks, and government savings banks, the West Indian peoples practise thrift and saving in many ways, ranging from actual hoarding of money hidden in the ground, tied in stockings or hidden in a mattress, where they receive no interest, to Su Su, Credit Union, Friendly Societies and Insurance.

PERSONAL BUDGETING

Suppose a man is working for $600 per month, has to pay rent of $150, light $15, phone $20, and wants to save $50 each month, then his personal budget would look something like this.

Expenditure for month		Income	$600
Rent	$150		
Groceries	200		
Transport	60		
Light	15		
Phone	20		
Hire purchase	30		
Pocket money	50		
Recreation	25		
TOTAL EXPENSES	550		
Savings	50		
	$600		$600

Now suppose the man was working weekly, say for $150 per week. Let us suppose that he had monthly bills to pay e.g. rent $150, light $15, phone $20, hire-purchase $30. His total monthly bill is $215. His budgeting should look something like the example .

Note that the $215 for monthly bills is paid out of the total of the savings ($268) giving him a monthly saving of $53.

Weekly budget	
Groceries	50
Transport	15
Pocket money	12
Recreation	6
TOTAL EXPENSES	**$83**
Savings per week	**$67**

Monthly budget

Total of 4 weeks expenditure	$332	Total income for month	$600

Bills paid monthly

Rent	150		
Light	15		
Phone	20		
H.P.	30	$215	
		547	
Total monthly savings		53	

| $600 | | | $600 |

Other forms of saving and thrift

SU SU
The word Su Su is of African origin and may have originated from the West African tribe Su Su. The people of this tribe practise a system of saving in turn. The Su Su tribe was heavily involved in the slave trade and in fact members of this tribe were brought to the Caribbean. It stands to reason that they took their customs and practices with them. The practice of Su Su, or saving in turn, is still very common among West Indian people, especially among the people of the working class.

In a Su Su, or Meeting Turn, a group of people, usually twelve if the meeting is monthly, more if it is weekly, decide to contribute a fixed sum (say $20) to a common pool. The pool is given to a different member in turn each month or week until each member has had a turn, then the Su Su starts all over again. In some cases, although not all, the person who runs or is in charge of the Su Su receives a percentage of the pool. The main advantage of the Su Su is that it is a form of planned saving, allowing members to purchase some needed commodity some time in the future by making small monthly or weekly savings.

THE CREDIT UNION
In the 1840s Frederick Raifferson established the first Credit Union which made a substantial contribution towards solving the dire needs of the German peasant farmers who were exploited by unscrupulous moneylenders. Almost one century later, in the 1940s, the movement came to the Caribbean, brought here by the Church, and catered mainly

for the needs of Church groups for a number of years. Today the movement has spread throughout the entire Caribbean and is recognised as one of the primary means of improving the economic and social well-being of the people. Some governments have even adopted it as the financial arm of the cooperative movement, which they are depending upon to improve the entire national economy.

What is a Credit Union?

A Credit Union is an organisation of persons, with a common bond, who pool their savings by depositing them in the Credit Union. These savings are then used to provide members with low cost loans in time of need. Legally a Credit Union is a Corporation chartered by some Government agency (the Registrar of Cooperatives) under special Credit Union Laws. The Credit Union is a business run and operated by volunteer leaders.

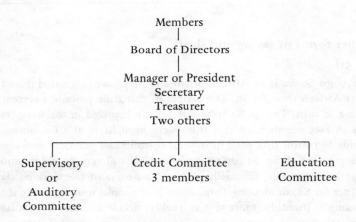

Structure and organisation of a Credit Union

A credit union is a true cooperative, ultimate control is in the hands of members who meet at least once a year to elect directors and committee members, review past operations and adopt policy for future operations. The rule is one member, one vote.

The board of directors, consisting of five members, is elected by all the members. The members of the board choose from within their group a president, vice-president, secretary and treasurer.

The credit committee, also chosen by members, is usually required to approve all loans except loans made to other Credit Unions, which must be approved by the board of directors.

166

The supervisory or auditory committee makes regular audits of the Credit Union's books and reviews actions of the directors and the credit committee to make sure that the law, the by-laws and the resolutions of the members are complied with. It reports its findings to the directors, the membership meetings and the Registrar of Cooperatives.

Benefits of a Credit Union

(a) It teaches people to save.
(b) It builds self-reliance and self-confidence.
(c) It provides members with a 'heightened spirit of enterprise', leading to improvement in a country.
(d) It assists in capital formation.
(e) It is a cheap source of loan.
(f) It provides a better standard of living for its members.
(g) It reduces the cost of living to its members.

Sources of capital

Traditionally the main sources of capital in the Caribbean, apart from personal savings which are generally too low for any worthwhile investment project, have been the commercial banks, e.g. Barclays, Trust Companies, e.g. Royal Bank Trust, insurance companies, or solicitors who invested the money of clients. Of course shares are sold on the local market and companies have used ploughed-back profits.

Recent additions to the above list could be central banks, national banks, development banks, e.g. Industrial or Agricultural Development Banks, and the Caribbean Development Banks.

Foreign development banks also play an important role in providing funds, especially for long-term government projects.

The above institutions can be said to be the main lenders in the money market and capital market as they exist in the Caribbean. The money market is the market for short-term capital finance to purchase raw materials and stock and to meet short-run deficits in revenue. The capital market is the market for long-term capital finance for long term projects, to build or expand a factory, or to invest in some industry.

The borrowers in the money market are (i) the government which borrows through the issuing of Treasury Bills or Government Debentures; (ii) investors, e.g. businessmen in the manufacturing industry, hoteliers in the tourist industry, merchants in the distributive trade and construction firms.

The main lenders in this market are the commercial banks, national banks and insurance companies. However, firms may borrow from suppliers through credit and from purchasers through advance payments, and from other companies.

In the capital market, such as it exists in the Caribbean, the borrowers are the same as in the money market. The lenders now include the Caribbean Development Bank and other foreign development banks and financial institutions. There is no active stock exchange for the buying and selling of shares, but companies do raise capital by public issues of shares and debentures, while governments float development bonds, e.g. National Development Bonds, or Housing Bonds. Company reserves are also used as a source of financing projects.

A STOCK OR SECURITIES EXCHANGE

A stock exchange is a market for the buying and selling of stocks, shares, and other interest-bearing securities including government securities. It is reputedly a free and perfect market subject to the laws of supply and demand. In the Caribbean context, a securities exchange should provide a means of investment of mainly short-term, but also long-term, balances. Stock exchanges exist in Jamaica and Trinidad. Barbados started a Securities Exchange.

Functions of a stock exchange

(a) It provides a ready market for securities, thus making securities more liquid than they would otherwise have been. This encourages more people to invest.

(b) It provides a good indication of the value of shares to buyers and sellers.

(c) It provides a basis for valuation of estate duties, and also an asset value to investors.

(d) Only shares of reputable firms are allowed quotations, thus the public can be confident that they are not being swindled when buying shares.

(e) Stock exchange securities are quickly and easily transferable; this makes the jobs of accountants, solicitors, executors and trustees easier.

Organisation of a stock exchange

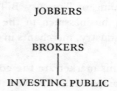

JOBBERS

|

BROKERS

|

INVESTING PUBLIC

The jobbers are the dealers or wholesalers of the stock exchange. They buy and sell shares. They generally specialise in certain classes of shares and deal only through brokers, not directly with the public. They make a profit (jobber's turn) by buying at one price and selling at another which is higher than the buying price.

The brokers are agents acting as intermediaries between jobbers and the investing public. They make arrangements for the purchase and sale of securities. Usually they charge a percentage of the money value of the shares changing hands, thus securing a brokerage commission.

The stock exchange has an account period of two weeks. This is the period of exchange dealing from one settlement day to another. Should a deal not be completed within that period a fee called a contango is charged to allow it to go over into another period.

THE BARBADOS SECURITIES EXCHANGE: A NEW EXPERIMENT
In the Barbados Experiment the functions of jobbers and brokers would be performed by the stock exchange itself which is made up of agents authorised to trade on behalf of clients. The exchange would deal in all shares except Treasury Bills, and it would be illegal for people to buy shares except through the Securities Exchange; the exception to this rule would be private company shares. In other words, the Barbados Securities Exchange would both regulate and control dealings as well as deal itself.

Companies wishing to receive a quotation must first of all be listed, secondly they must supply the exchange with all information which is price sensitive. The value of the shares would be what the exchange is prepared to pay for them. It is proposed that dealings will take place twice weekly and on the last day of each period quotations will be published. The settlement period will be three days. This is to discourage speculation, to make securities negotiable and to satisfy people who want to off-load shares.

The principle behind the exchange is to encourage a greater flow of money into business and not into banks.

Questions

1   Describe how a Su Su is run.
2   How is a Credit Union organised?
3   What are the benefits to be derived from a Credit Union?
4   Why is it necessary to manage one's money?
5   What is a stock exchange? How would the establishment of a stock exchange assist Caribbean businesses and investors?

21 Insurance

Origin of insurance and assurance

Insurance has its origin in antiquity and can be traced back to ancient Greece and Rome. It is said that when slave galleys were chartered by traders, the owners and masters of the vessels would agree to compensate the traders if the ship or its cargo was lost at sea. The Lombards, famous as bankers and traders, introduced the word 'polizza', a promise, into the world of insurance, and the contract of insurance became known as the 'policy'. Insurance is based on the probability of an event happening, and the sole purpose is to make good losses by providing monetary compensation.

Insurable and non-insurable risks

Non-insurable risks are risks which cannot be assessed in value. The probability may be incalculable, or they may be risks which are against the public interest or illegal. In business, non-insurable risks are risks such as failure to anticipate market demand correctly and failure to manage the firm efficiently.

Insurable risks are those risks which can be assessed in value or of which the probability can be assessed. In business, insurable risks are the non-economic risks such as fire, hurricanes, accidents, etc.

General principles of insurance

The main purpose of insurance is to provide a common fund to which people will make contributions, and which can be used to make good losses suffered by unfortunate members. For example, in a particular town of, say 100,000 people each person may contribute $10.00 per year against the event of a hurricane. The pool will be $1,000,000 at the end of the year. Suppose a hurricane were to take place and a number of houses were to be blown away, with total damage estimated at

$500,000. Each of the damaged houses would be compensated for according to the value of the damage done to the house by the hurricane. The remaining $500,000 would be carried over to the next year as a reserve fund, so that at the end of the second year the fund would be $1,500,000. Of course, administration costs would be subtracted.

To secure insurance one must first fill out a proposal form. Generally an agent or life-underwriter (in the case of life assurance) would provide such a form. The proposal form is really a questionnaire which seeks to gather all relevant information from the applicant. Information given on this form forms the basis of the insurance policy or contract to be issued later by the company if the application is accepted.

An applicant is advised to read the form carefully, and to make sure he understands all the questions asked before completing the proposal form, as relevant information not disclosed by the insured might invalidate a claim for compensation.

If the proposal is accepted by the company, it would then issue a policy. The insured person is required to pay a premium weekly, monthly or annually, according to the type of insurance taken. The premium is based on the calculated probability of the event happening.

In some cases, e.g. in motor car insurance, the whole premium must be paid when making the application. A cover note is then made out by the insurers to give temporary cover until the official policy is issued.

PRINCIPLES
Utmost good faith, or Uberrimae fidei
The principle of 'Utmost good faith' is one of the most important principles governing an insurance contract. The term implies that all vital facts likely to affect the attitude of the insurance company must be disclosed by the insured. In life assurance, for example, the insured should disclose any history of heart disease in his family, as this would affect the attitude of the insurer and also the premium to be paid. The principle also applies to the company whose representative should reveal all relevant facts pertaining to the policy to the insured.
Indemnity
All insurance is based on the principle of indemnity, which means to make good or to restore the insured to his or her former position. For example, if A had insured his property for an amount of $50,000 in the event of a particular event happening, and the event did occur causing damages of $20,000 to A's property, then A would receive compensation of $20,000, enough to make good his losses and nothing more. A must not be made better off but must be restored to his former position. The exception to this rule is Life Assurance.

INSURABLE INTEREST

Before anyone can insure a property against a possible event or risk, he must have an insurable interest in the property. This means that he must be in the position to suffer a loss or damage in the event of the event happening. For example, a man cannot insure his neighbour's house, even if he thought the house, built of wood, was a fire risk to his own. What he can do is insure his own house.

PROXIMATE CAUSE

Suppose Mr. Jones's house was insured against fire. If a fire started as a result of Mr. Jones's kitchen stove exploding then he would have a case against the insurance company as the proximate (closest or immediate) cause originated within the house. If however, a gas tanker parked next to his house exploded, causing his house to burn, then he would not be able to claim from his insurance company as the proximate cause did not originate within his house. He could, however, sue the owners of the gas tanker.

SUBROGATION

If A's car was hit by B's, then A would have certain legal rights against B since B was responsible for hitting A's car. Now suppose A's company took care of the damage, then by the law of subrogation A's insurance company would be entitled to any compensation A received from B.

CONTRIBUTION

If a person has insured identical risks on the same property through a number of companies, then the amount of the loss is shared between the insurance companies. This prevents the insured from receiving the full compensation from each company and so making a profit.

Types of insurance

Insurance can cover lives or it can cover property. Life and non-life insurance are usually carried out by separate companies. In the Caribbean most of the companies are of foreign origin although a few large local companies exist. Recently governments have passed laws to regulate and control the foreign companies. Some governments have even entered the insurance business themselves.

LIFE ASSURANCE AND ENDOWMENT

There are two main types of life assurance policies.

(a) **Whole life,** where a fixed sum is payable on the death of the insured.

(b) **Endowment,** where a stated sum is payable after a number of years or on the death of the insured, whichever occurs first. Endowment policies represent a form of saving in addition to providing assurance. These policies usually include a 'with profits' clause, which means that the policy holder will receive a small share of the company's profits, once the shareholders of the company have received a minimum dividend on their investment. These policies can be 'surrendered' after a minimum number of years has elapsed, then the company will repay part of the total premiums paid. Any bonuses that may have been earned may be forfeited. Policies with a cash surrender value can be used as security for a loan.

Age next birthday	Period for which premiums are payable Cost for $1,000				
	Whole Life	20 years	25 years	to age 60	to age 65
21	$ 7.80	$13.10	$11.30	$ 8.90	$ 8.50
22	8.10	13.50	11.60	9.30	8.80
23	8.40	13.90	12.00	9.70	9.20
24	8.70	14.30	12.30	10.10	9.60
25	9.00	14.70	12.70	10.50	9.90
26	9.40	15.20	13.50	11.10	10.40
27	9.70	15.60	13.50	11.50	10.80
28	10.10	16.10	13.90	12.10	11.30
29	10.50	16.60	14.30	12.70	11.80
30	10.90	17.00	14.80	13.30	12.30

Extract from table for calculating whole life assurance (figures are hypothetical)

MARINE INSURANCE
There are several types of policies in marine insurance.
1   **Time specified** e.g. six months.
2   **Voyaged** Cover is only for one trip.
3   **Time and voyaged** Cover is for one trip and for a specified time, e.g. Guyana to Barbados, two weeks.

4 **Floating** Cover is the same as for regular voyages.

5 **Valued** The value is agreed beforehand.

6 **Unvalued** The losses are assessed afterwards.

MOTOR INSURANCE

There are two main types of policies in motor insurance.

1 **Comprehensive** This covers all risks and injuries to driver and third parties and assessed damage to vehicles or property at the time of the accident.

2 **Third-party risk** This is compulsory by law. Third-party insurance includes claims from passengers travelling in the insured vehicle and from any other persons injured as a result of an accident, and also any claims for damage to another vehicle or the property of third parties. The insured cannot claim for damage to his own vehicle.

BUSINESS INSURANCE

Insurance is very important to every business regardless of its size. Damage to or loss of buildings and equipment by fire or flood means the loss of business and profits while the premises or machines are being repaired. Business insurance covers this type of risk and is of great benefit to a company and its customers.

Types of business policies

1 **Fire** Fire policies cover the insurance risk of both the building and the contents. There is generally a 'loss of profits' clause on the fire risk policy, because the profitability of the company is affected while it is closed for business. Fire policies usually cover damage due to flood, earthquakes, hurricanes and other acts of God. The premium paid for a fire insurance policy will depend on the value of the property insured and the risk involved.

2 **Burglary** This type of policy compensates the firm for loss resulting from goods being stolen and damage to property through an actual break-in to the premises as opposed to simple stealing.

3 **Employers' liability and public liability** These policies cover accidents occurring to employees and customers through the negligence of the employer or the firm.

4 **Plate glass insurance** This policy covers the cost of replacing large shop windows. It also covers serious injury to staff or customers from the breakage of such windows. These policies also include a 'loss of profits' clause as there is a loss of advertising display resulting from the breakage.

5 **Bad debts** These policies cover the risk which businesses face that money owed to them will not always be paid. For example expor-

ters run the risk of non payment for goods shipped to foreign customers, therefore some governments provide policies called Export Credit Guarantees to protect local exporters.

6 **Goods in transit** Loss or damage to goods which are being transported from one place to another by sea or air can be covered by this type of policy.

ACCIDENT AND HOSPITALISATION POLICIES
Apart from life insurance, these are two of the most common policies used in the Caribbean. They offer protection in the eventuality of accident with a doubling or even tripling of the insured sum due to death by accident. Hospitalisation plans offer coverage of hospital expenses up to a period of 90 days in most cases. The cost of surgical operations and maternity expenses are also covered.

Recent trends in the insurance industry

The most recent trend has been the setting up of local life underwriters associations. These associations, apart from providing avenues for training life underwriters for the Charter Life Underwriters Certificate, perform other functions.
(a) They aim to create and maintain the goodwill of the public, to promote cooperation and goodwill, and in all ways to promote the best interest of legal reserve life insurance.
(b) They try to advance public knowledge of legal reserve life insurance and its uses. (Legal reserve life insurance is the legal requirement that insurance companies deposit a specific sum of money, in reserve, as a security, to satisfy the needs of policy holders against total loss should the company fail.)
(c) They work to promote the adoption and application of the highest standards of ethical conduct in the profession of Life Underwriting and the business of insurance.
(d) They work to increase the knowledge of agents concerning legal reserve life insurances, its uses and its sale.
(e) They also try to provide community services and to form enduring friendships.
   Recently, a Caribbean Life Underwriters Association has been formed.

Benefits of insurance

(a) It protects manufacturers and businessmen against personal risks such as accidents at the plant, fire, burglary, etc.

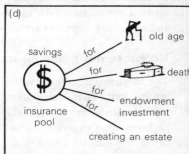

Benefits of insurance

(b) It protects exporters and shippers against the hazards of the sea, or damage or loss of cargo.

(c) It protects householders against such risks as loss of property due to fire, flood, hurricanes, etc. It also provides them with protection against a penniless old age.

(d) It is a form of saving and investment, e.g. endowment policies.

(e) It is a source of capital for business and householders, e.g. mortgages or loans to companies.

(f) It creates an estate to be passed on to relatives at death.

Questions

1 How does insurance benefit (i) businessmen; (ii) a private individual?
2 Explain (i) indemnity; (ii) insurable interest; (iii) proximate cause; (iv) utmost good faith.
3 How does life assurance differ from an accident policy?
4 Find out about any recent trends in insurance in your country.

22 Consumer affairs

Being an informed consumer

The word production means the creation of goods and services for use by the consumer. (See the figure on page 6.) When these goods and services have been used up we say they have been consumed, for example when we burn fuel in our cars, or when we have a haircut. Consumption, then, refers to the process of using goods and services by households and firms: in the case of households, for their own satisfaction, and in the case of firms, to produce other goods.

Every consumer seeks to maximise his satisfaction — he seeks to ensure that every penny spent brings him the greatest satisfaction. In order to do this he must have some knowledge of the technical capacity of the goods or services available to him, and he must know the exact price of each good and service. In other words he must buy intelligently. But is intelligent buying possible in today's world? Intelligent buying is becoming increasingly difficult as new inventions and new industries are introduced at a rate that does not give the consumer time to adjust to change. Furthermore, commodities seem to get more complex, for example electrical goods. The consumer today is faced with such a wide range of different items and brands that it is difficult to decide which of these items and brands give greatest satisfaction. Today's consumer is bombarded by advertisements on radio, television and in newspapers. These hard-sell methods make it difficult for consumers to decide what is best for them. Finally, as communication and transportation increase we come into contact with people whose standards of living are higher than our own. As a result, we grow to want and demand things that we do not really need. Increased income also tends to cause a demand for more and more goods, especially luxury items.

These are the problems which today's consumers face and which hinder intelligent buying. What can consumers do to counteract these problems and so maximise satisfaction? A consumer must use his good judgement when planning to buy an item. Each purchase must be judged as to whether it will give more pleasure than something else the consumer might have bought instead. The purchase of an item must be guided by the relationship between the need or want for that item and the possible needs or wants for others.

Here are some suggestions for good decision-making when purchasing an item.
(a) Would you rather buy this item than another which you could buy for the same amount of money?
(b) Which dealer should you go to?
(c) What quality of merchandise do you want to buy?
(d) What price are you willing to pay?
(e) Should you pay cash or buy on credit?
(f) Is the item really needed now, or can it wait until later?
(g) If you purchase this item, what other important items will you have to forego?

Earlier in the chapter it was stated that a consumer must have some knowledge of the technical capacity of the goods and services available to him. From where can he get such information? There are numerous sources to which he can turn.

SOURCES OF TECHNICAL INFORMATION
Below is a list of helpful sources of information for the consumer:
(a) labels on products;
(b) advertisements;
(c) product testing agencies;
(d) newspapers;
(e) magazines;
(f) radio;
(g) television;
(h) experts or specialists;
(i) consumer organisations;
(j) government organisations.

From these sources, the consumer obtains information in the following ways.

Labels They provide written information about the product, such as:
(a) what the product is made of;
(b) what the size or capacity is;
(c) how to care for the product;
(d) when and where it was produced;
(e) expiry date;
(f) any necessary warnings about the product.

Advertisements Some advertisements are designed to give information

178

about a product. They should tell the consumer:

(a) what the product is;
(b) how it is made;
(c) what it will do.

When studying an advertisement, the consumer should ask himself:

(a) Is it giving facts which can be used for comparison with other products?
(b) Is the advertisement only making vague and general claims that really say nothing about the product? For example, 'Buy Manchilo — they're better!' The question to ask is, 'Better than what?'

Reports of testing agencies In the Caribbean there are no private testing agencies. However, in some islands there are government-run testing agencies. Consumer organisations in the region may obtain valuable information on foreign goods for their members by writing to Consumers' Research Inc., and the Consumers' Union of the United States Inc. These agencies test goods and report on their quality.

Magazines and newspapers Magazines and newspapers often carry articles of help to consumers. Magazines such as *Consumers Guide* and *Automechanic* can give consumers useful information on household appliances and cars.

Using radio and television Many radio and television stations carry programmes which are of help to consumers with regard to the use of products. Stations carry programmes which inform the public about new inventions, product safety, care and use of products and shopping tips.

Information from businesses Some firms provide their customers with booklets and brochures on a variety of consumer topics, for example safety. They also give information concerning the products they sell: how they are made, and care of the products.

Specialist advice In many instances, as when buying a new item, especially one of a technical nature, it is wise to get expert advice on what to look for. For example when buying a new or used car one should seek the advice of a mechanic.

Consumer information provided by Government The Ministries of Consumer Affairs in most Caribbean islands provide consumers with information on many consumer goods. Such information includes:

(a) grade and size of goods;
(b) prices of consumer items;
(c) desired standard of goods;
(d) health and safety requirements.

Other functions of the Ministry of Consumer Affairs are:

(a) the regulation and control of prices;

(b) the setting of standards or quality control;
(c) the enforcement of regulations governing labelling;
(d) the enforcement of regulations governing production and sale of food, beverages and use of drugs.

Consumers should make use of all the above sources of information if they are to buy intelligently.

Shopping for the best buy

Having discussed how an informed consumer can make a more sensible decision about what to buy in order to gain the greatest satisfaction for money spent, particularly regarding technical information, we can now turn to other aspects which he should consider carefully. The following general rules would also help him spend wisely. He should:

(a) take his time;
(b) buy at the right time;
(c) compare prices and service;
(d) look for genuine 'sales';
(e) avoid impulse buying;
(f) examine carefully what he buys;
(g) be familiar with brand names;
(h) look for unit pricing.

Consumer rights and responsibilities

Many consumers are ignorant of their rights and responsibilities regarding consumer affairs. However, such knowledge is very important if consumers are to get the best value for money spent. The responsibilities of a consumer should include the following points.

1   **A responsibility to be informed** This is perhaps the most important responsibility of a consumer. As a consumer you must make sure that you obtain and make use of all information available to you. How many consumers read the labels on products they purchase? To be an informed consumer, you should keep abreast of information concerning the many goods and services available on the market.

2   **A responsibility to be honest** As a responsible consumer, you must be as honest with business as you expect business to be honest with you. For example, you should be as quick to tell the cashier that you have received too much change as you are to say that you received too little.

3   **A responsibility to complain in a reasonable manner** If as a con-

sumer you are dissatisfied with the goods or service which you have received, you should make your complaint to the merchant in a reasonable way. Be sure you first have a genuine cause for complaint, for example make sure that you have followed the directions for using the product before complaining. When you are sure you have good cause to complain, do so in a calm manner, avoiding an angry or threatening approach.

4   **A responsibility to report unethical business practices** As a responsible consumer, your responsibility extends to all other consumers. If you should encounter unethical business practices, you have a responsibility to report them to the proper authorities so as to protect other unsuspecting consumers.

Let us now turn to consumer rights. As a consumer you have a right to:

1   **Be informed** In other words you have the right to be given the correct information needed to make a sensible choice.

2   **The right to safety** You should be protected from goods and services that are hazardous to health and life.

3   **The right to choose** Consumers should be assured of the availability of a variety of goods and services at competitive prices.

4   **The right to be heard** Consumer interests should be fully considered by the Government when laws are being made and enforced.

Money management

Wise management of money is necessary if householders are to gain the greatest satisfaction from their money incomes. Money management does not mean penny pinching, doing without things and restricting your enjoyment. It means getting the most that you can for your money. It means careful planning, saving and spending. It means deciding what you want and what you can afford.

Let us consider some guidelines for good money management.

(a) Set goals based on what is important to you.
(b) Rank goals in order of priority.
(c) Provide for basic needs.
(d) Save money for future expenses.
(e) Make wise decisions when you buy.
(f) Get the most out of the things you buy by using them properly.
(g) Live within your income.

THRIFT
The word thrift means saving or saving ways. It means refraining from spending now so as to be able to purchase something in the future.

Included in a consumer's budget or financial plan should be some provision for saving. Saving does not mean piling up money for its own sake, but putting money aside for specific purposes. People generally save for emergencies, for example in case of loss of job, or illness; to buy something they want in the future, such as a home; and to provide for the future, especially for old age. The amount saved depends upon the income of the saver, and on the reasons for saving.

What are the avenues open to a householder or family for saving? The figure below shows some of the traditional ways of saving.

Commercial Banks

Su Su or
Meeting Turn   Credit Union
                              SAVING
Insurance   Friendly Societies

Trust Companies

Saving institutions (banks and others)

BUYING ON CREDIT

Most consumers today purchase articles through credit. This means that they buy something today and agree to pay for it another time. There are various ways of obtaining credit. Among them are hire-purchase, credit trading, check trading and credit cards.

Hire-purchase

Hire-purchase enables the purchaser to take possession and enjoy the use of the articles bought, while the merchant continues to own them until full payment has been made. A written contract called the hire-purchase agreement is entered into between the purchaser and merchant. This is a contract to hire the goods specified in the agreement, and gives the hirer the option to acquire ownership when all instalment payments have been made.

Credit trading

In credit trading the buyer owns the goods at the time of purchase, but pays later. Some large stores offer budget accounts to selected customers, who agree to pay fixed monthly sums against the outstanding balance on their accounts. Providing regular payments are made, a customer may be permitted to buy between six to eight times the amount of his monthly instalments. The full amount is normally repaid in six months or a year, depending on the agreement.

In credit sales under deferred terms, a deposit and regular instalments are made by the customer, but ownership of the goods passes immediately to the buyer. The goods cannot be repossessed if the purchaser defaults, but the seller may sue for recovery of the amount due.

Check trading

In check trading the members of the group agree to pay weekly or monthly subscriptions to collectors who call at the homes of members. On payment of the first instalment, a member is given a check or voucher which entitles him to make purchases from specific retailers up to twenty times the amount of his instalment payment.

Credit cards

Credit cards allow the holders to draw cash (up to a stated amount) from any branch of the bank issuing the card; to present a personal cheque in payment of credit accounts at shops, hotels, etc; and to purchase goods on credit from any supplier who is paid by the bank issuing the card. The bank then charges the cardholder in due course.

The advantages of credit buying to consumers are:
(a) they are able to have immediate use of the goods whilst still paying for them;
(b) people with small incomes find it easier to pay weekly or monthly instalments than to save the full amount before purchasing the goods; and
(c) the customer is in a strong position should the goods prove to be unsatisfactory.

However, there are disadvantages to be considered.
(a) Consumers are tempted to purchase goods beyond their means, and, in many cases, agree to monthly or weekly payments which they cannot meet.
(b) Consumers pay a higher rate of interest when buying on credit. They are also losing the interest which would accrue if they were to place their money in a bank deposit or savings account until the amount necessary for the purchase was saved.
(c) The customer does not always have the same choice of quality as when he pays cash. In other words, he may have a limited choice when buying goods on credit.

Why do consumers demand or buy certain goods? The demand for a particular good depends firstly upon the personal taste of the consumer (for example he may prefer oranges to grapefruit), secondly on the number of alternatives available (for example the demand for tea depends not only on the customer's taste for tea, but also on the availability of substitutes for tea, such as coffee and chocolate) and thirdly on the price of the good in question, and also on the price of the substitutes (for example if tea costs $4.00 for a four-ounce tin, but four ounces of coffee cost $3.00, given that the consumer has no special preference for either tea or coffee, he will go for the cheaper product). The size of the income of the consumer plays an important part in deciding how he spends his money, for example the larger the income the more luxury items that will be demanded. In addition the availability of and the terms of credit also influence the buying patterns of consumers. The more credit that is available, and the easier the repayment terms the more purchases that will be made.

Buying locally made goods

In many Caribbean countries consumers are urged to purchase locally produced goods in preference to foreign-made goods. Why should consumers be encouraged to purchase the former rather than foreign goods which may be cheaper and also of a better quality? The answer is that when locally produced goods are purchased the country concerned benefits in the following ways.

(i) Local production is further encouraged and so the number of jobs is greater.

(ii) The country saves on foreign exchange, i.e. the importation of foreign goods declines and so there is less need for foreign exchange.

(iii) Savings on foreign exchange mean an improvement in the country's balance of payments.

Thus when consumers buy locally, jobs are created, money remains within the country and can then be used to build more schools, roads, etc., and economic growth is stimulated.

Questions

1 What do you understand by the term consumption? Why is consumption important to an economy?

2 What are the problems which consumers face?

3 How can consumers' associations assist consumers?

4 Class project. Find out about agencies (government and private) in your country which assist and protect consumers. Find out the functions and responsibilities of these agencies.

5 Of what importance is a 'Buy Local' campaign to your country?

6 Distinguish between: hire-purchase, credit trading, check trading and credit cards.

23   International trade

The Caribbean region has been historically dependent upon international trade. For centuries the region has been producing primary products such as sugar, cotton, bananas, spices, oil and bauxite for export to foreign countries and importing large amounts of foodstuffs and manufactured goods.

Since about 1960 the Caribbean as a whole has been unable to produce sufficient primary products to pay for the commodities we import. The prices of the manufactured goods we import and the price of fuel, mainly oil, keep rising steeply. These conditions produce certain effects on our economies which may have serious repercussions on the standard of living.

International trade may be defined as trade between nations. It consists of the selling (exporting) of goods and services to other countries and the purchasing (importing) of goods and services from other countries.

Reasons for international trade

International trade exists mainly because of three factors. Firstly, climate differences: the climate throughout the year is not the same the world over, different places have spring and summer, or rainy and dry seasons at different times of the year, tropical countries have summer all year round while temperate countries do not. Different crops thrive under different climatic and soil conditions.

Secondly, nature did not endow each country with an equal amount of natural resources. While some countries are rich in natural resources, e.g. fertile land, forest, rivers, minerals, others have little or none at all.

Thirdly, specialisation and technological know-how: countries tend to specialise in the production of those goods and services for which they have the greatest relative advantage, or the least relative disadvantage. Further, some countries have developed a greater degree of specialisation and technology than others.

THE LAW OF COMPARATIVE ADVANTAGE

Let us assume that we are dealing with two countries, A and B, and two commodities, sugar and motor cars, and that there is a production schedule for a given outlay in each country as follows:

A can produce 30 units of sugar or 15 motor cars.

B can produce 15 units of sugar or 10 motor cars.

Country A, it would appear, has an advantage over country B both in the production of sugar and of motor cars, as both sugar and cars can be produced more cheaply in country A than in country B.

Trade can take place if A's advantage over B is not proportionally the same for both commodities. A will tend to specialise in the production of the commodity in which it has the greatest comparative advantage, or least comparative disadvantage. In our example the cost of production of sugar is half that of cars, while in B it is two-thirds that of cars. A's comparative advantage is greater in the production of sugar and she will thus tend to specialise in the production of sugar leaving B to specialise in motor cars.

BENEFITS OF INTERNATIONAL TRADE

As stated above, international trade comes about partly as a result of international specialisation. One of the most important results of this specialisation is an increase in production or output; more commodities are produced for distribution world wide.

The world becomes one market as a result of international trade. This means that within individual countries more large scale production, using the division of labour and other methods or mass production, could take place, since production is not simply for the small home market. From this we see that international trade may cut down on unemployment within individual countries.

Another benefit of international trade is that it tends to improve the standard of living of a country. Apart from the facts of increased exports and employment, it makes available to citizens a wider variety of goods and services than would normally be obtained if there were no international trade. It may even prevent famine and starvation in some countries because scarce goods can be obtained from abroad.

International trade prevents formation of, or where they already exist, reduces the effect of, local monopolies, since these monopolies would face competition from imported products which may be cheaper and of better quality.

Think of some other benefits of international trade and discuss them with your class.

The terms of trade

'The terms of trade' is an expression for the rate or ratio at which one commodity is exchanged for another.

In the example on comparative advantage, above, the terms of trade would be the ratio of exchange between sugar and motor cars. The exact rate of exchange between the two commodities which will prevail in the end will depend on the relative elasticities of supply and demand of the two commodities.

Generally, the country producing the commodity with the less elastic demand will be better off than the country producing the commodity with the more elastic demand.

The terms of trade can usually be measured as follows:

$$\frac{\text{Export unit value index}}{\text{Import unit value index}} \times 100$$

If the prices of imports rise relative to the prices of exports, then the terms of trade are said to have become less favourable or to have moved against the country concerned since, to obtain the same quantity of imports as before, a greater volume of exports must be sold abroad. An increase in the terms of trade index means that the terms of trade are more favourable, export prices have increased relative to import prices.

An improvement in the terms of trade may mean:
(a) more imports can be obtained for a given quantity of exports;
(b) improvements in the balance of payments;
(c) better incomes for workers in industry;
(d) an increase in employment.

Points (b), (c) and (d) are very important to Caribbean countries which are essentially exporters of primary products. It must be pointed out that here we are speaking about real increases in the terms of trade and not increases due mainly to inflated prices.

Barriers to international trade

In discussing international trade, we assumed that free trade existed between countries. However, in practice this is not the case. There are numerous barriers which obstruct the free movement of goods and services between countries.

CUSTOMS DUTIES OR TARIFFS
These are imposed:
(a) to raise revenue; they are easily collected and they do not usually distort trade a great deal. This is the main source of revenue to

many Caribbean islands;

(b) to protect local industries against outside competition by making foreign goods more expensive, compared to locally manufactured goods, for example the common external tariff of the Caribbean Common Market;

(c) to provide protection against dumping; i.e. goods are sold much more cheaply in the importing country than in the exporting country;

(d) to improve the balance of trade by imposing taxes on imported commodities;

(e) to reduce unemployment by encouraging home production and making foreign commodities very expensive;

(f) to protect key industries, e.g. agriculture;

(g) to reduce the consumption of rum and tobacco (undesirable commodities).

QUOTAS AND LICENCES

Sometimes customs duties have little effect on the importation of goods. Governments therefore restrict the amount imported to a definite quantity. This quantity is called a quota.

Another method of restricting importation of goods is by placing certain commodities under licence. This means that before the commodity can be imported, the importer must first obtain a licence from government. The government can thus delay the importation for as long as they think possible, or even refuse to issue a licence. Quotas and licences are used by many Caribbean governments.

EXCHANGE CONTROL

Exchange controls are used by a number of Caribbean governments. When exchange controls are imposed all earnings of foreign currency or claims to foreign currency have to be handed over to the government or its agent (the Central Bank), which alone has the power to authorise withdrawals from this fund for the purpose of paying for imports, foreign travel and capital movements.

Exchange controls are imposed:

(a) to limit the amounts of foreign currency spent on imports;

(b) to control the export of capital;

(c) to distinguish between the importation of essential and non-essential goods and services;

(d) to discriminate against those countries whose currencies are 'hard' and to favour those countries whose currencies are 'soft'.

PHYSICAL CONTROLS

Some Caribbean countries have placed complete bans and embargoes on the importation of certain goods.

The balance of payments

The balance of payments account sets out to identify and record transactions made between the residents of a country and non-residents to provide information suitable for analysing economic relations between that country and the rest of the world. Balance of payments accounts record three basic types of transactions:

(a) flows of real resources: goods, services and property income;
(b) changes in foreign financial assets and liabilities that arise from transactions;
(c) transfer payments, which are the counterpart of real resources or financial claims to, or received from, the rest of the world without any *quid pro quo*.

The balance of payments must always balance since goods bought must be paid for in some way, and because the double entry system of accounting is used so that the sum of the credit entries must be equal to that of the debit entries. Positive or credit entries are recorded for outflows of real resources (export of goods and services) and financial items (decreases in foreign assets and increases in liabilities); debit entries are made for inflows of goods and services and financial items.

The balance of payments transactions are divided into three areas.

1 **Current account transactions** These cover imports and exports of goods and services and transfers.
2 **Investment and other capital** These include public and private sector long-term and short-term capital transactions, and other capital transactions.
3 **Official financing** This covers changes in the reserves, net borrowing from the International Monetary Fund, net transactions with overseas monetary institutions and Government borrowing for balance of payments support.

The balance on current account shows whether or not *earnings* from the outflow of goods and services (exports) and receipt of transfers from abroad exceeded *payments* for the inflow of goods and services (imports) and transfers to non-residents.

The basic balance, which is the balance of current account and long-term capital transactions, is intended to measure long-term tendencies in the balance of payments and to show a balance that has not been distorted by fluctuations, speculative or easily reversible factors.

189

Visible trade refers to transactions (imports and exports) of tangible goods, e.g. consumer durables.

Invisible trade refers to the export and import of services, e.g. tourist expenditure, shipping, banking, insurance, transportation charges, etc.

The balance of trade refers to the balance on visible exports and imports. It is called favourable when exports exceed imports and unfavourable when imports exceed exports. An unfavourable balance on visible trade may be offset when the invisibles are taken into account, thus giving a surplus on the overall balance of payments on current accounts.

METHODS OF CORRECTING AN ADVERSE BALANCE OF PAYMENTS

The obvious course to take to correct cumulative adverse balance of payments problems is to attempt to reduce imports and/or to increase exports. In order to reduce imports, a number of restrictive measures may be employed. These include the introduction of tariffs, quotas, special licences and exchange controls, all of which have been discussed earlier.

A country wishing to increase exports must:

(a) offer incentives and subsidies to local manufacturers;

(b) encourage foreign manufacturers to invest locally by providing them with factory space, and other incentives (tax holidays, etc.);

(c) extend maximum credit facilities to all industries and merchants in the export trade;

(d) improve local marketing skills, and sponsor overseas trade exhibitions;

(e) ensure harmonious industrial relations;

(f) offer export credit guarantee facilities to manufacturers and exporters;

(g) take deflationary measures, e.g. restrict the money supply, increase taxes, reduce government spending.

DEVALUATION

Governments facing adverse balance of payments problems may also devalue the local currency. This means reducing its value against other currencies. This should lead to higher exports since the goods of the country are now cheaper in relation to other goods. However, it also means that more has to be given for the same amount of imports. This may lead to a drop in imports depending on the elasticity of demand of goods imported.

To tide the country over the period of balance of payments problems the government may decide to approach the International Monetary Fund for a loan, or to draw down on its SDR (Special Drawing Rights). However, before this can be done the country must be prepared to follow the conditions for reconstruction which the IMF prescribes. Alternatively a country may decide to borrow from friendly countries and neighbours, or beg for gifts from abroad, or to import on credit. Importing on credit may only postpone the problem to a later date.

Central Bank of Barbados

Credits		Debits	
Exports	149,035	Imports	468,519
Services	287,599	Services	108,248
Government	10,930	Government	8,299
Merchandise freight and insurance	2,631	Transportation	25,058
Transportation	40,723	Travel	16,450
Travel	169,054	Investment income	16,268
Investment income	7,769	Other services and income	42,146
Other services and income	56,501	Transfer payments	11,420
Transfer payments	36,828	Government transfers	6,745
Government transfers	6,599	Private transfers	4,675
Private transfers	30,229	Total debits	588,187
Total credits	473,462	of which goods and services	576,767
of which goods and services	436,634	Goods and non-factor services	544,129
Goods and non-factor services	407,314	Current balance	114,725
		of which goods and services	140,133

Current account of Barbados, 1975 ($000)

Summary

1	Current account		11	Balance FN official	
2	Visible trade	− 363,230		financing (4 + 5 + 9)	− 6,354
3	Invisibles	+ 271,185	12	Allocation of SDRs	
4	Current balances (2 + 3)	− 92,045	13	Gold-tranche subscription	
5	Capital account		14	Official Financing	
	(6 + 7 + 8)	59,472	15	Net transactions with	
6	Long-term capital	+ 38,894		overseas monetary	
7	Short-term capital	+ 10,039		authorities	35,135
8	Other capital	+ 10,539	16	IMF	15,135
9	Errors and omissions	26,219	17	Other	20,000
10	Basic balance (4 + 6)	− 53,151	18	Reserve movements (−Increases/+Decreases)	−28,781

Barbados balance of payments for 1977

Questions

1 Why do nations trade with each other?
2 Is foreign trade beneficial to Caribbean territories? Give reasons for your answer.
3 How do the terms of trade affect your country?
4 What is the balance of payments? Why is it so important to Caribbean countries?
5 What measures could a country take to correct constant balance of payments problems?

24 The role of governments

We have examined business organisations and the business environment, marketing and the aids to trade. We must now look specifically at the role of governments. What are the functions of governments? What part do they play in stimulating and assisting trade and business? How do they control the economy and protect the rights of consumers?

The functions of governments

These may be divided into four main groups.

(a) The provision of law and order and of defence: the upkeep of the legislature and the courts of justice; the maintenance of law and order within the state; the provision of facilities for defence; diplomatic representation to safeguard its interests from external dangers and to discharge its international responsibility.

(b) The encouragement and control of certain sectors of the economy for social, strategic and economic reasons. The government may provide support to agriculture and industry through the provision of subsidies, financial assistance, advisory services, promotion agencies and dissemination of information. It may even participate directly in industry through state ownership and public corporations.

(c) The provision of social services: the provision of education, health, welfare and culture.

(d) Responsibility for the overall state of the economy: the maintenance of a high and stable level of employment; the encouragement of a maximum rate of economic growth and productivity; the preservation of the country's foreign reserves; the management of the national debt, ensuring a healthy balance of payments position.

It should be pointed out that a certain amount of overlapping is unavoidable between the functions, for example, see (b) and (d) above.

Functions	Expenditure
Provision of public services	Administration, justice, police, defence, foreign embassies and missions.
Control of public and private sectors	Agriculture, transport, commun-cations, industry, and other economic services
Social policy and community services	Education, health, welfare and culture, roads, water, pensions
Control of economy	Public debt, local government events, miscellaneous

THE BUDGET

At the beginning of each financial year a government presents its budget. The main purpose of a budget is to decide how much money the government plans to spend for services to its citizens and how it intends to collect the money from them to pay for these services. The budget spells out the amount of taxes which the government needs to collect to cover its expenditure, the manner in which the tax is to be collected, the goods and services on which taxes will be placed, and in some cases subsidies and grants which will be offered to certain sectors to stimulate economic growth.

TAXATION

A tax is a compulsory payment to be made by a citizen to the government, for which he receives no direct benefit in return. It is generally held by economists that a tax system should follow certain rules.

1 **Equality of sacrifice** Each subject should contribute towards the costs of government according to his ability, in relation to the income which he receives.

2 **Certainty** The tax which each citizen must pay ought to be certain and not decided arbitrarily. The manner, time, and quantity of payment ought always to be clear and plain to the contributor.

3 **Convenience** Taxes should be levied at the time and in a manner which is most convenient to the contributor.

4 **Economy** A tax should be so constructed as both to take out and to keep out of the pockets of the contributor as little as possible over and above what it brings into the public treasury.

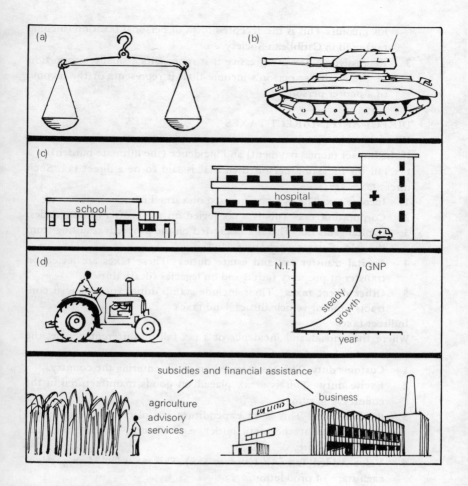

Functions of a government
(a) Justice
(b) Defence
(c) Social Services
(d) Support for agriculture and business

A tax may take one of three forms.

1   **Proportional**   Every taxpayer pays the same proportion of his income by way of tax, so that the wealthier taxpayer pays more in absolute terms, but only the same percentage of his income.

2   **Progressive**   A taxpayer with a higher income should pay not only a larger absolute amount in taxes, but also a larger proportion of

his income. This is the accepted form of personal taxation (income tax) used in Caribbean Society.

3   **Regressive**   A tax is regressive if it represents a smaller proportion of the wealthier person's income than it represents of the income of a poorer person.

DIRECT AND INDIRECT TAXES

Direct taxes

If the impact (actual payment) and incidence (the ultimate burden) of a tax fall on the same person then that is said to be a direct tax. Such direct taxes are:

1   **Income tax**   This is a tax imposed on earned income.
2   **Corporation tax**   This is a tax levied on the profits of companies.
3   **Capital gains tax**   This is a tax levied on the proceeds resulting from the sale of assets e.g. houses, land.
4   **Capital transfer tax and estate duties**   These taxes are levied on transfer of property (gifts) and on legacies (death duties).
5   **Other direct taxes**   These include stamp duties (on financial contracts), motor-vehicle duties, land taxes.

Indirect taxes

Where the impact and incidence of a tax fall on different people, the tax is said to be indirect. Such taxes are:

1   **Customs duty**   This tax is levied on goods entering the country.
2   **Excise duty**   This is a tax placed on goods manufactured in the country, e.g. rum.
3   **Purchase tax**   This is an expenditure tax placed on certain consumer items at the retail outlet, e.g. tobacco, petrol, wines and spirits, furniture.
4   **Value Added Tax** (*Ad Valorem* Tax)   This tax is levied on goods at each stage of production.

REASONS FOR TAXATION

We have seen that taxation is needed in order to finance government expenditure. However, there are some other objectives which governments hope to achieve by means of taxation. These objectives are:

(a) to exercise overall control of the economy in order to achieve full employment. To do this governments use taxation to influence consumption, including consumption of undesirable commodities, savings and investment, and to vary the relationship between its own expenditure and revenue by means of budget surplus or deficit.
(b) to promote economic growth by giving allowances for investment and taxing re-invested profits at a lower rate.

(c) to modify the influence of the price system in order to protect pioneer industries, and to develop vital industries.

(d) to improve the balance of payments by imposing duties to restrict imports.

(e) to achieve greater equality in the distribution of wealth and income, by means of progressive income tax and capital gains and transfer taxes.

Government and business

We have just seen that government has responsibility for the promotion of economic growth, ensuring a level of full employment and maintaining a healthy balance of payments position. Government policy then has serious implications for business within the country. The government should always try to maintain a strong and efficient business environment. In order to assist business, governments usually set up ministries with direct responsibility for commerce, trade and industry. However, other ministries such as those of health and labour are also concerned with businesses.

In most Caribbean territories governments assist trade, commerce and industry by providing various services.

(a) Infrastructural services: energy (electricity), water, roads, transportation and communication facilities.

(b) Market intelligence and information about trends in both local and overseas markets.

(c) Incentives and subsidies to infant industries and exporters.

(d) Export promotion assistance by holding overseas exhibitions.

(e) Export credit guarantee facilities.

(f) Trade agreement with foreign countries, e.g. Lome, Canada and the U.S.A.

(g) Providing factory space and facilities.

(h) Providing easy credit and low interest loans to local businessmen.

(i) Providing training, management assistance to small businessmen and, through their ministries of education, providing business education courses and training schemes for businessmen, and technical training for people involved in industry and for those hoping to enter industry.

(j) The setting up of institutes of standards.

(k) Providing research facilities into new products and finding ways of improving existing industries.

(l) Setting up machinery to ensure that there are harmonious labour relations within the country. This is essential if business is to grow and be productive.

197

(m) Recently governments in the region have initiated National Insurance Schemes to which both workers and employers contribute. National Insurance provides sick benefits, maternity benefits and old age pensions for workers, and it is hoped that unemployment benefits will later be paid to workers.

CONSUMER PROTECTION
In nearly all the countries in the region responsibility for consumer protection comes under the Ministry of Consumer Affairs. Among other things the Ministry is responsible for:
(a) control and supervision of prices;
(b) giving advice to consumers;
(c) food policy legislation;
(d) hire purchase and credit control legislation (as it affects consumers);
(e) quality control and weights and measures;
(f) fair trading practices.

The Ministry of Health is also concerned with consumer protection. The Ministry through its legislation and inspection ensures that premises used by consumers conform to certain stated health standards, that all food and beverages served are fit for human consumption, and that the servers themselves are medically fit. In this way the Ministry of Health protects the interest of consumers.

Nationalisation and local and foreign investment

A recent trend in the Caribbean is for governments to nationalise certain industries. Nationalisation is the taking over of an industry or firm by the state and placing it in the hands of a public corporation. Nationalisation, then, means ownership and control by the state.

The questions we must ask are, why is it necessary for the state to control certain industries, and what benefits are to be derived from nationalisation? From the point of view of the Caribbean, nationalisation may result in the following benefits.
(a) Ownership and control of national resources would ensure that profits remain in the region, and are used for the further development of the region.
(b) Certain social benefits could be provided for the community. For example, the nationalisation of transportation may lead not only to a cheaper transport system, but to a more efficient system.
(c) The formation of private monopolies could be prevented.

(d) The efficiency of certain firms could be improved, e.g. where there is need of capital for expansion.

(e) Employment could be provided for the masses.

(f) Certain key industries which are vital to economic development would be sure to remain in the hands of the state.

Some governments in the region prefer not to nationalise but speak of joint ownership, with government having a controlling interest. By use of this method, governments with majority interest can gain control and direct the policy of business without having to take over fully, which would entail the setting up of a corporation board, and the payment of compensation to the nationalised business.

Another recent trend is to encourage both local and foreign investment. Local businessmen are encouraged to invest locally by the provision of incentives, e.g. credit facilities, protection for pioneer industries, provision of factory space, etc. Foreign investors are also encouraged by the provision of tax holidays, double taxation agreement, allowing the repatriation of profits, provision of factory space, etc.

The encouragement of both local and foreign investment is part of the policy to speed up industrialisation of the region, and in so doing speed up economic growth and development, and provide a better standard of living for the people. The result of more local and foreign investment would be:

(a) the eventual elimination of unemployment;

(b) increasing the technical skills and know-how of the working population;

(c) providing training for future managers and entrepreneurs;

(d) a strengthening of our foreign reserves, and elimination, or correction of balance of payments problem;

(e) increasing the Gross National Product;

(f) improving the standard of living and reducing poverty.

Questions

1 What are the major functions of a government?

2 By what methods may a government finance its expenditure?

3 Why do governments impose taxes? List the different forms of taxation.

4 How does a government assist businessmen?

5 Why do governments nationalise industries?

25 National income

National income and national product

The National Income or the National Product is the total output of a community over a period of time, say one year, measured in terms of the money value of the total production of goods and services.

Why do we need to know the quantity of goods and services the community produced over a year? First of all the government must have some idea or estimate of the state of the economy: the total flow of wealth (goods and services) produced, distributed and consumed by the economy as a whole. This allows them to compare the flow of goods and services in one year with that of another, and so determine the rate of economic growth. National income figures can also be used to compare the economic position of different countries.

Secondly, national income figures could give some indication of the standard of living of the people in the country from year to year, and again when compared to that of people in other countries.

Thirdly, national income figures indicate the rate at which the nation's income is growing and so assist government in planning the economy, businessmen in planning future investment, and trade unions in determining whether to ask for wage increases.

National income may be measured in two ways or from two different approaches.

THE FLOW-OF-PRODUCT APPROACH

In this approach we simply add together all the consumption dollars spent for final goods and services. For example the community would have produced bread, bananas, tables, cars, and services such as tyre repairs, haircuts, etc. The public would have spent dollars on these goods and services, so now we simply calculate the sum of the yearly flow of these goods and services.

Price of a loaf × number of loaves + price of a banana × number
of bananas + price of a chair × number of chairs + price of a car
× number of cars + price of a tyre repair × number of tyre
repairs + . . .

We use market prices because they are the best reflectors of the relative
desirability of diverse goods and services. Market prices are responsible
for the allocation of resources and determine what goods and services
are produced.

THE FACTOR EARNINGS OR INCOME APPROACH

In this approach we add the dollar earnings of the factors of production.
Businesses are paying the public for factor services, e.g. land receives
rents, labour receives wages, capital receives interest and enterprise
receives profits. Wages, rents, interests and profits are the costs of production.

The two approaches are identical — National Product is identical to
National Income. The reason is due to the fact that in the second
approach profits are included along with rents, wages and interests.
Remember that profit is what is left over from the sale of a product
after the other factors have been paid. Profit is that extra that is needed
to make the two approaches identical.

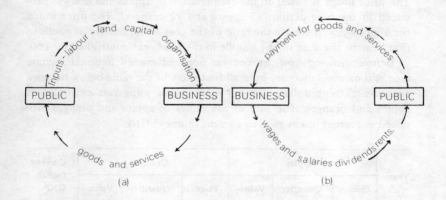

The circular flow of income, goods and services
(a) Public funds provide input for business, business provides goods
    and services
(b) Business pays wages, rents, interest and profits to public funds,
    public funds pay for goods and services

REAL NATIONAL INCOME

Ordinarily, we use money as the measuring rod for national income. However, money as a measuring rod is very unreliable as the value of money tends to vary during a given time period. To correct the unreliability of money as a means of measurement, we introduce an index number of prices. The table below shows how we compute a price index. The index number of prices is used to deflate 'money' or 'nominal national income' converting it into 'real national income'.

Year	Prices		Output		Cost of 15 apples and 12 oranges	Price index
	Apples	Oranges	Apples	Oranges		
1970	$1.00	.50	10	10	$21	$\frac{21}{30} \times 100 = 70$
1971 (base period)	$1.20	$1.00	12	12	$30	$\frac{30}{30} \times 100 = 100$
1972	$1.40	$1.50	14	14	$39	$\frac{39}{30} \times 100 = 130$

Computing a price index

The price index is based on the combination of apples and oranges produced in the base period (15 apples and 12 oranges). The price index for a given year is simply the ratio of the cost of the bundle of goods in that year to the cost of the bundle in the base year, multiplied by 100.

Before showing how we convert nominal money national income into real national income, we shall first show in the table below how we compute current dollar (money) GNP, again using our examples of apples and oranges. The sum of the values of apples and oranges produced in current prices gives us current (money) GNP.

Year	Apples			Oranges			Current Dollar GNP
	Price	Quantity	Value	Price	Quantity	Value	
1970	$1.00	10	$10	.50	10	$ 5	$15
1971	$1.20	15	$18	$1.00	12	$12	$30
1972	$1.40	20	$28	$1.50	14	$21	$49

Computing current dollar GNP

Current or money GNP divided by the price index and multiplied by 100 gives constant or real GNP as shown in the following table.

Year	Current GNP	Price Index	Constant $ Real GNP	
1970	$15	70	$21.40	$15 ÷ 70 X 100
1971	$30	100	$30.00	$30 ÷ 100 X 100
1972	$49	130	$37.70	$49 ÷ 130 X 100

Computing constant dollar (real GNP)

At each stage of production some value is added to the basic raw material; this is reflected in the final sales price. Using the value-added approach is another method of arriving at a total for GNP.

Stages of production	Sales price	Final product	Value added
Farmer Produces and sells raw food	.30	—	.30
Food processer Processes food and sells ingredients to packager	.55	—	.25
Packager Combines ingredients, packages mix and sells to supermarket	.80	.89	.25
Supermarket Sells to consumer	.89	.89	.89
	$2.54	$.89	$.89

Value added approach to avoid 'double accounting'

Real income and output *per capita*

An important use of national income accounts is to measure the change in output and incomes from year to year. Such comparisons require some adjustments of GNP or GNE (Gross National Expenditure). For example the output of one year may be larger than the output of the previous year, but if the larger measured output was due to price increases, physical output would be no greater than the previous year. It is for this reason that adjustments must be made if we want to compare the two years. In such a case we use a 'GNP deflater', which is the price index introduced above.

However, even if real GNP increased by the same amount in each year, it does not mean that individuals' real income also increased by the same amount. Increases in real output per person will depend on the relative rates of increase in population and in real output (see the table below).

Gross National Expenditure					
Year	Money GNP (000,000)	Year 2 (100)	Real (base year) GNP (2) 000,000	Population 000	Real GNP *per capita*
1	39,646	72.4	54,741	18,238	3,001
2	94,450	100.00	94,450	21,569	4,379
3	289,859	222.7	130,160	23,941	5,437

Note that although real GNP grew by 72 per cent between years 1 and 3 the real GNP *per capita* rose by only 46 per cent in the same period, because the population grew by 18 per cent between years 1 and 3.

Other national income accounts
GNP is only one of several important national income accounts. We can derive other accounts from GNP by subtracting and adding various amounts.

Net national product
To get net national product we subtract an amount allowed for capital consumption or depreciation from GNP. The NPP represents the country's output of final goods and services less depreciation of its capital goods. For example:

GNP	$3,500
Depreciation (allowed)	− 700
NPP	$2,800

204

National income

National income is the sum of all income components — interest, rent and profits and proprietors' income and compensation. In its simplest form NI = NNP less indirect business taxes. For example:

NPP	$2,800
Indirect business taxes	− 300
NI	$2,500

Personal income (PI)

National income is not the same as income received. Personal income is calculated by subtracting profits retained by businesses, business taxes and social security contributions, and adding transfer payments. For example:

NI	$2,500
Social security contributions	− 200
Business taxes	− 75
Undistributed profits	− 50
Transfer payments	425
PI	$2,600

Disposable income (DI)

We have seen that personal income measures income received by households, but this is not the same thing as income available for consumption or saving. We must now subtract the personal taxes on income, inheritance and personal property paid to the Government by householders. For example:

PI	$2,600
Personal taxes	− 400
DI	$2,200

Disposable income may be broken down into its component parts. For example:

Consumption	$1,860
Interest paid by consumers	60
Personal saving	280
DI	$2,200

National income and standard of living

Earlier in the chapter we said that national income figures give some indication of the standard of living of a country. The standard of living of a country may be defined as the sum total of material goods and services which people consider fitting and proper for themselves. We divide the national income by the population and the resulting figure, called *per capita* income, gives us an idea of the standard of living of a country.

We must be very careful, however, when using this *per capita* income figure for the purpose of comparison. In fact we should take the following into consideration when using *per capita* income figures for the purpose of comparing standard of living between countries:

(a) rises in the general price level from one year to another and in one country as compared with another;

(b) the quantity of consumer goods and services enjoyed by consumers, and the actual amount of money after taxes which they have to spend; also whether or not increases in national income were due to increases in capital goods produced, and therefore an increase in exports;

(c) how income is distributed in the countries or the years under review;

(d) whether the rise in income came about through working longer hours, under inferior working conditions or with more housewives at work;

(e) how great a part government expenditure on defence played in increasing national income.

The standard of living of a country then is not only determined by the national income per head of population, but is also influenced by:

(a) the distribution of wealth in the country;

(b) the quantity and quality of consumer goods and services, including number of phones, newspapers, etc;

(c) the conditions under which people work and travel to work, and the social services (provided by government) available to the people.

The question is now, what are the factors which determine a country's level of production. In answer we shall summarise some of these factors.

1 **The natural resources** These include mineral deposits, sun, wind, climate, fertility of soil and fish in the sea. How well these are utilised and developed could determine the standard of living of a country.

2 **The nature of the people, especially the labour force.** It is generally accepted that the standard of living will be higher, the greater the proportion of workers to the number of dependants and the longer

their working hours. The skills, training and education, inventiveness, health, energy, adaptability and ability to cooperate and organise themselves are also very important attributes which should be possessed by the labour force.

3   **The capital equipment available**   Equipment, e.g. machinery, is needed for combining with natural resources and the labour force. The use of adequate capital equipment can greatly increase the material wealth of a country.

4   **Factors of production**   Of very great importance is how these factors are combined. This requires great managerial and entrepreneurial skills.

5   **Technical resources**   Research and invention plus technical know-how, are also essential if we are to make proper use of our natural resources, and available capital equipment. However, in countries such as ours there tends to be a lack of technical know-how, research and inventiveness.

6   **Political stability**   In order to encourage saving and investment, especially in long-term capital projects, a stable political system and government is required.

7   **Financial stability**   Stable, or unfluctuating, terms of trade are also important. The terms of trade affect the rate of exchange between goods, e.g. the amount of manufactured goods we are able to get in exchange for our sugar exported to the E.C.C. If the terms of trade remain constant or if they increase in our favour, then our standard of living may increase.

8   **Foreign aid**   The amount of developmental aid we can get from abroad can lead to improvements in the standard of living.

Growth and development

The economic growth of a country is determined by the growth of its national income, or increases in the total output of goods and services, taking into account inflation and changes in population. A country which has a rapid rate of growth will also enjoy a rapidly rising standard of living, if the benefits of growth are allowed to reach domestic consumers.

Development is frequently confused with economic growth; thus, aggregate figures which have been accepted as satisfactory indications of economic growth are sometimes regarded as adequate indicators of development, even though the concepts of development and economic growth may be based on different evaluations of social phenomena. The concept of development involves normative judgements. For example, in a developing society development also requires the building of just societies, eliminating poverty, and providing adequate conditions for the development of the human personality.

For the purpose of this book, we shall define development, in the Caribbean context, as the reduction and eventual elimination of poverty, the reduction and eventual elimination of unemployment and under-employment and the removal of inequalities in the distribution of wealth and income. Poverty may be regarded as the set of conditions which prohibits people from being able to afford certain minimum levels of nutrition, shelter, clothing and medical care.

FACTORS AFFECTING ECONOMIC GROWTH AND DEVELOPMENT
Rate of investment
It is generally accepted in economics that savings equals investment. By saving we mean not spending, i.e. not using one's income on the purchase of consumer goods.

The rate of new capital accumulation is the most important factor affecting the rate of growth. A country must devote a large proportion of its national income to its wealth-creating potential, or capital equipment, and in order to do this, the rate of saving within the country must increase.

The rate of increase of the working population
Capital equipment by itself will not produce additional wealth unless there exists the required amount of man-power to operate the equipment. Thus, the rate of increase in the working population is another important factor. Also, the labour force should be mobile: willing to move from one job to another or one area to another.

Technical training
Economic growth requires not only a large labour force, but also a highly trained labour force, consisting of technicians, technologists and experts in other fields, e.g. management. This means that there must be adequate investment in education.

The role of government
This is also very important in stimulating economic growth and development. Government fiscal (taxation) and monetary (credit) policy should be geared towards stimulating and encouraging saving and additional private investment. Such a policy should favour the transfer of income from consumption to investment.

Government expenditure
This also plays an important part in stimulating economic growth and development. Public expenditure should be invested in fields which assist future output.

Balance of payments

An essential requirement for economic growth and development is a healthy balance of payments position. If the balance of payments of a country is persistently unfavourable, and the country's foreign reserves are limited, then economic growth and development will be hampered. Economic growth also depends upon a heightened spirit of enterprise, self-reliance, and self-confidence among the population of the country. The absence of such attitudes among the population could be a hindrance to economic growth and development.

Questions

1 What do you understand by the term national income? How is it measured?
2 How does national income relate to the standard of living?
3 What factors determine a country's standard of living?
4 Distinguish between economic growth and development.

26   Problems of development

In the last chapter we saw that economic growth is determined by the growth of a country's national income, while economic development has to do with the eliminating of poverty, the eventual elimination of unemployment and underemployment, and the removal of inequalities in the distribution of wealth and income. We also saw that it is possible for a country to have economic growth, or increases in its national income, but no economic development. In this chapter we shall examine the problems of economic development. We shall try to explain some of the reasons behind the slow pace of economic development found in the Caribbean region, and some of the steps that have been taken to try to remedy the situation. We shall also look at some of the international organisations which give assistance to developing countries.

Dualism

One of the most striking features of development in the Caribbean, and one that will continue to present a problem for some time, is what the economists call technological dualism.

Dualism is the division of the economy into two distinct and radically different sectors, one technologically advanced and the other technologically retarded. In the advanced or modern sector are found the petroleum, other mining, large-scale manufacturing or tourism enclave, large-scale mechanised plantation agriculture and the transport, finance, insurance, trading and other services associated with these activities. In the retarded sector or traditional sector are found peasant agriculture, handicraft and cottage industry and very small-scale manufacturing industries, and again the services related to these undertakings.

In the modern sector the typical operation is frequently the corporation or the multinational, simply because of the capital requirements involved. The technology is usually as advanced as modern science can make it. Productivity per man-hour or per man-month is accordingly high. In the traditional sector, techniques are themselves traditional, sometimes centuries old, (e.g. outmoded methods of peasant agriculture) and highly labour intensive. Productivity is correspondingly low.

The wages in the modern sector are usually much higher than those in the traditional sector. This puts pressure on the economy in two ways. Firstly, there is distortion in the wage structure of the economy, as trade unions tend to force up wages in the traditional sector to match that offered in the modern sector. Secondly, labour is attracted away from the traditional sector to the highly paid modern sector.

Unemployment and underemployment

One of the greatest hindrances to development in the Caribbean is the dual problem of unemployment and underemployment. Underemployment refers to the number of people working less than a normal working week and seeking additional work and people doing a job which is below their ability level. This also happens among peasant farmers who have insufficient land. When a man is doing less than a normal week's work but is not seeking additional work, this is referred to as disguised unemployment. Other characteristics of unemployment in the Caribbean are seasonal unemployment and unemployment caused by droughts and crop failures.

Unemployment in the Caribbean is not a simple problem. It relates to several factors of both an economic and a social nature. It is firstly, a reflection of the large proportion of the labour force in agriculture and of the phenomena of technical and regional dualism.

Secondly, there is the high rate of growth of the labour force resulting from rapid increases in the population in the 1950s and continuing growth in the population. Thirdly, the wage structure of Caribbean economies has had an important effect on unemployment. In the Caribbean the structure of the economies (dualism) and trade union activities which are modelled on those in highly developed and industrialised countries tend to exert a lot of pressure to push up wages in both the technically advanced sectors and the lower-productivity sectors. This tends to aggravate the unemployment problems.

Finally, education, both formal and informal, has also affected employment in the Caribbean. Formal education has tended to place too much emphasis on academic subjects and little or no emphasis on technical skills. The result is that secondary school-leavers are extremely choosy about the level of remuneration which they will accept. Thus they remain unemployed rather than accept a job or salary which is beneath their expectation.

Informal education, especially the type one gets from the mass media (both the press and the electronic media) creates a set of perceptions, values and aspirations which are both irrelevant and harmful to the region. These values and aspirations relate to the consumption patterns, aspirations and standards of highly industrialised economies such as the United Kingdom and North America, with which we are bombarded daily in the mass media, and which our economies cannot maintain.

Population and migration

One of the most urgent concerns of Caribbean government today is that of maintaining a reasonable balance between the resources of the region and the number of people among whom these resources must be shared.

POPULATION

Within the last two decades there has been a new awareness of the connection between population rates and economic and social development, i.e. the effect of population growth on such problems as employment, urbanisation, food supply, education and the standard of living in general. Political and social leaders have been calling for methods to regulate pregnancies and so lower the birth rate, thus controlling the rate of growth of population.

An increase of population may come about as a result of:
(a) increases in the birth rate;
(b) lowering of the rate of mortality (death rate);
(c) net migration, i.e. increases in the number of people coming to settle from abroad (immigration).

If the birth rate exceeds the death rate, we speak of net natural increases.

The incredible acceleration in the rate of growth of the population in the Caribbean is not so much a result of increases in the birth rate, but, rather, an improvement in the conditions of life which has led to decreases in the death rate. The drop in death rate is due to improvements in public sanitation, in nutrition and medical care.

In the Caribbean the total population was less than 10 million in 1920 and more than 20 million in 1960. The population for Carifta, now Caricom countries, in 1970 was 4,366,000. For the total commonwealth Caribbean, other territories and the Guianas it was 25,389,000. Population problems, though, are not just a question of size, but also of composition. The proportions of each age group in a population, and

212

the balance between the sexes are also important statistics because different age groups make different demands on a country's resources. As an example, the number of pre-school children this year determines the number of school places needed in the next few years, and the number of children too young to work and the number of elderly people place a burden on the economically active population.

In the Caribbean, it is estimated that more than 10% of its population is aged between 15 and 21 and that about 42% of the total population is aged under 15 years.

Problems caused by population increase

Firstly, the increase in growth rates means that any economic gains made will be eroded by the increasing population. This means that territories in the region seeking to industrialise and to raise the levels of living find that while they are exerting all their efforts to increase output of goods, they are barely able to provide enough for maintaining the additional numbers at the same level of living.

Secondly, as a result of an expanding population, more pressure is placed on governments to provide social facilities, medical care and other amenities, all of which must be paid for. This places a strain on government revenue and resources and may mean increase in taxation to the population.

Thirdly, as seen above, the age distribution of the population creates its own problems, the chief of which has to do with finding employment for the young school-leavers coming into the labour market. In fact the chronic unemployment situation in the Caribbean is a result of the population explosion of the 1950s. The unemployment situation could lead to social unrest among the population.

To sum up we can say that unless birth rates can be sharply curtailed and the growth rates of the population held in check all our efforts at industrialisation would be futile, as any gains will be just enough to maintain present position; also, a great part of available labour and capital must be diverted from savings and investment to feed, clothe, educate and provide jobs for a large number of young people.

MIGRATION

One way of curtailing the increases in population is by means of migration to foreign countries. In fact, many countries in the Caribbean escape problems due to population increases because of migration to Panama, Cuba, the United Kingdom and North America. However, most of these avenues are now closed or partly closed. Moreover, migration itself created problems for Caribbean industrialisation and development, as those who migrated were the better educated and skilled people who were needed at home to assist in the industrialisation programme. A new type of migration is taking place in the Caribbean. It is the drift of people from the rural areas into the towns. This is called rural migration. The movement is part of the process of urbanisation, or the growth and spread of towns. The reasons for this movement are as follows:

(a) the attraction of town life;
(b) the promise of employment in the city;
(c) the mechanisation of plantation agriculture in some territories and the poor state of peasant agriculture in others;
(d) increase in the rural population and the scarcity of jobs in the rural area.

Again, this movement is putting pressure on authorities in the cities and on governments who must provide more housing space, better sewage disposal and sanitation facilities, more school places, and must spend more on police and detention facilities.

Some problems of industrialisation

Most countries in the region are concentrating on industrial development as a means of promoting economic development. Industrialisation is seen as an important factor or strategy in the war against poverty. Through the development of industries the countries of the region hope to provide employment for their increasing labour force, to cut down on their massive import bills, by providing import substitutes, to generate foreign reserves through exports of locally manufactured goods, to own, control and direct the use of local resources.

The industrialisation programme of the region is however faced with a number of obstacles.

(a) There is a lack of indigenous capital and a dependence on foreign capital and investment. The reason for lack of indigenous capital is due to what is called the vicious circle of poverty.

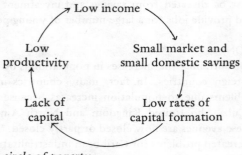

The vicious circle of poverty

214

(b) Much industrial development in the Caribbean involves enclave activities with little or no linkage effects with the rest of the economy and a low level of absorption and diffusion of technological skills.

(c) There is scarcity of entrepreneurial skills and a low level of technology and technically trained people in the region.

(d) The calls for greater public control and participation by some countries have turned away foreign private investment.

(e) Traditional approaches to industrial development which no longer meet the needs of the present situation continue to be employed in most countries.

(f) Marketing problems such as meeting the product standards of foreign consumers and market restrictions imposed on local subsidiaries of multinational companies prevents countries from penetrating the international markets.

(g) Adverse balance of payments problems and large debts owed to foreign countries have affected the adaptation and use of imported technology which is capital intensive.

(h) There is a low level of industrial mentality.

(i) There is the disadvantage of being a late-comer in the area of industrialisation.

The dependence on foreign capital has been most disadvantageous to our economy, because of the concessions we have had to offer to attract such capital. List the concessions offered to foreign investors in your country.

The role of education

The governments of the Caricom member states attach great importance to the role of education in promoting national and regional development. They realise that education can be a real force for changing the social and economic order and thus improving the quality of life in the individual member states of the region.

Why is education so important to economic development? Several reasons have been advanced for the importance of education in economic development. Firstly, the lack of education leads to 'economic backwardness' which is manifested in:

(a) low labour efficiency;

(b) factor immobility;

(c) limited specialisation in occupations and trade;

(d) a deficiency in the supply of entrepreneurship, customary values and traditional social institutions that minimise the incentives for economic change.

We might also add that the economic quality of the population remains low when there is little knowledge of what natural resources are available: the alternative production techniques that are possible; the necessary skills; the existing market conditions and opportunities; and the institutions that might be created to favour economising effort and economic rationality. Further, there is under-investment in human capital. The rate at which additional physical capital can be productively utilised will be limited since technical, professional and administrative people are needed to make effective use of material capital.

Since expenditure on education competes with alternative productive investment, it is essential to determine what proportion of national income should be devoted to education, and to establish priorities, within the educational system, for various forms of education and training possible. If we are interested in speeding up economic development, the emphasis should be placed on vocational and technical training and adult education rather than on a greatly expanded system of formal education. The most critical manpower requirements tend to be for people with a secondary education who can be managers, administrators, professionals, technicians, or sub-professional technical personnel. Also deserving of high priority is the infusion of new skills and knowledge into the agricultural sector, in order to achieve a system of modern agriculture and to improve the quality of labour in agriculture. Education for agriculture may also provide a way of curtailing the rural migration to the towns as rural school-leavers may be encouraged to take up work in the rural sector, and may allow them to be innovators in rural agriculture.

Finally, if education is to play a meaningful role in development in the broadest sense, manpower surveys may furnish a useful basis for the determining of the principal skill shortages and what types of training activities should be emphasised.

Caricom

Caricom was formed in an attempt to solve some of the region's development problems.

REGIONAL TRADE

Regional trade, or trade between the islands of the Caribbean, existed for centuries. It began soon after the islands were colonised and has continued ever since. The islands and Guyana buy and sell commodities such as rice, timber, ground provisions, fruit and manufactured goods, asphalt, rum, sugar and spices from each other.

216

Find out and make a list of these goods which your country or island sells regionally, and those it buys regionally.

REGIONAL TRADING AGREEMENT

On the 1st May, 1968 the first major regional trade agreement in recent times came into being. The agreement known as CARIFTA, Caribbean Free Trade Association, had as its main objective the freeing of trade among the participating countries. Under CARIFTA 90% of inter-regional trade was freed of import duties and quantitative restrictions, with special arrangements being made for the less developed countries to impose duties on imports from the more developed countries when similar industries in their own territories seemed threatened by these imports.

The next significant step was the establishment of an Economic Community Common Market. In October 1972 at Chaguaramas the seventh Heads of Government Conference decided to create a Caribbean Community which would have three areas of activity:

(a) economic integration through the Caribbean Common Market;

(b) common services and functional cooperation;

(c) the coordination of foreign policy among the independent countries.

Before going on let us give some definitions.

A free trade area exists when the tariffs and other trade barriers between countries are completely removed, but the level of tariffs against third countries (countries outside the free trade area) differs from one member country to another.

A customs union goes beyond a free trade area in that tariffs against third countries are unified; there is a common external tariff and common protective policy.

A common market is a customs union in which there is also free movement of labour and capital between member countries. There is no arrangement for the free movement of labour and capital in the Caribbean Common Market.

An economic community is a common market with a certain amount of coordination of economic, financial and monetary policies between member countries. An economic union is not only a common market, but also has common fiscal, financial, monetary and other economic and social policies between the member countries.

The Caribbean Common Market is the instrument for economic integration in the Caribbean community. Under the Common Market Agreement, the members have agreed to a Common External Tariff and

217

Common Protective Policy, the harmonisation of fiscal incentives to industry, a policy for the location of industries in the less developed countries and the development of regional integrated industries.

THE COMMON EXTERNAL TARIFF AND COMMON PROTECTIVE POLICY

The aim of the tariff is to achieve some measure of harmonisation among the various tariff arrangements in the region. It is also an important policy instrument to protect and develop the region's industries and redirect consumption habits. It is so constructed as to apply low rates of duty on import raw materials, intermediate products and capital goods, and higher rates on goods which can be produced within the region. The Common Protective Policy provides for quantitative restrictions to be applied by national governments in order to promote industrial and agricultural development.

FISCAL INCENTIVES TO INDUSTRY

The harmonisation of fiscal incentives to industry seeks to achieve some uniformity in the approach to measures for encouraging industry and to provide an advantage to the LDCs in their efforts at industrial promotion within the community. It makes provision for the following concessions:

(a) tax holidays of up to ten years in the case of the MDCs (in Barbados it is a maximum of eight years);
(b) export allowances;
(c) tax exemption of dividends;
(d) duty-free entry of raw materials required for industry.

In order to qualify for the above concessions an industry has had to have a certain amount of value added locally. In the MDCs the requirement was 50% local value added while in the LDCs the requirement was 40%. A new Process Criterion has now been drawn up.

THE RULES OF ORIGIN GOVERNING INTRA-REGIONAL TRADE

The new rules of origin by which goods will be held as originated within the Common Market and therefore entitled to free access to the entire regional market were agreed by the Common Market Council of Ministers in April 1976. The rules were to take effect on 1st January 1977, but reservations by the LDCs caused a delay in its implementation. Under the new rules, eligibility for Common Market treatment depends more on the extent of the manufacturing or processing operations performed within the Common Market than on the origin of the materials which are used in such manufacturing or processing.

Basically the rules provide that where a product is produced from imported materials or components, then the manufacturing or processing operation performed within the Common Market must result in a change of classification under the Brussels Tariff Nomenclature between these imported starting materials and components and the finished product.

The rules also require, for certain goods, the performance of specified manufacturing or processing operations, the utilisation of materials, wholly of Common Market origin, commencement of production within the Common Market with materials or components in a specified primary form and a temporary percentage value, an added requirement but without the facility of the Basic Materials list.

The Basic Materials list is a list of raw materials which, though imported from outside the Common Market, is considered to have originated within the region, for purposes of the value added criterion.

THE CARIBBEAN INVESTMENT CORPORATION
This corporation has the function of ensuring the promotion of the industrial development of the LDCs. The emphasis is on agro-based industries. The CIC can invest only in the smaller territories, the main objective being to supplement and complement the work of the CDB, and in particular to make equity participation. The headquarters of the CIC is located in St. Lucia.

REGIME FOR CARICOM ENTERPRISES
The Regime for Caricom enterprises was established in May 1976. The Regime is to permit the registration and incorporation of regional companies.

A Caricom Enterprise is defined as a regionally owned and controlled company which may engage in production of Common Market origin goods or provide services: (i) in specified areas; and (ii) in such sectors of the economy as Council may from time to time determine.

A regionally owned and controlled company means that the company is one in which, in the opinion of the authority, nationals of at least two member states exercise management and control by beneficially owning shares carrying between them directly or indirectly the following rights:
(a) the right to exercise more than one-half of the voting power in the company;
(b) the right to receive more than one-half of any capital distribution in the event of the winding up or of a reduction in share capital of that company;

219

(c) the right to receive more than one-half of any dividends that might be paid by that company.

A company must be approved by the Authority, under the terms of the agreement, to be considered a Caricom Enterprise. The Caricom Enterprise is a new regional corporate entity, a new form of business organisation to further the objectives of regional integration. Its basic aim is to use the financial, human and natural resources in the region in jointly owned ventures for the implementation of high priority projects, and to assist in the movement of investment capital between member states and particularly into the LDCs.

The idea is that a legal body will be incorporated in the member countries. This will facilitate the transfer of currency, the purchase of land and the movement of Caricom personnel in connection with the business of the Enterprise.

REGIONAL INDUSTRIES

The Caribbean Community aims at promoting and encouraging industrial development in the region. Efforts have therefore been made at the allocation of industries among the LDCs. This means that an allocated industry assigned to a particular country would enjoy special benefits, such as market protection or tax concessions, to enable that industry to cater for the total market identified.

An alternative approach has been the joint establishment of industries among territories. This has become a priority for the common market in both industrial and regional projects. The Oils and Fats Agreement is perhaps the best example, to date, of regional industrial cooperation with integration at all levels, including production and marketing.

The Oils and Fats Protocol is concerned with commodities such as copra and coconut oil. The prices of these commodities are fixed under these agreements so that the regional Marketing Boards and the Coconut Industry Boards have some indication of the prices to be offered to their farmers to stimulate production.

THE AGRICULTURAL MARKETING PROTOCOL

This protocol is designed to promote rationalisation of agriculture in the region. It seeks to do this by regular allocations of surpluses of specific agricultural commodities within the region and the fixing of prices thereof.

BENEFITS OF THE CARIBBEAN COMMUNITY

(a) Industrial and agricultural development is facilitated in the member countries.

(b) Industrial and agricultural specialisation is facilitated.

(c) Help to prepare local industries for exporting manufactured goods to the outside world.

(d) To secure the coordinated development of agriculture, industry, tourism and other sectors of the economies of member countries.

(e) The bringing about of structural transformation by creating backward and forward linkages.

(f) Coordination of certain economic policies, e.g. fiscal, monetary, financial and exchange rate policies.

(g) The adoption and application of joint coordinated actions and common policies in relation to outside countries.

BARBADOS' TRADE WITH CARICOM COUNTRIES

Period	Imports				Exports			
	Jam.	T.T.	Guy.	Other	Jam.	T.T.	Guy.	Other
1978	15.0	56.6	9.3	11.1	7.5	31.2	3.1	22.3
1979	25.4	89.8	8.6	13.0	5.2	37.0	3.1	30.9
1980	21.2	146.5	9.8	13.0	18.6	52.4	2.2	58.5
1981	28.2	132.7	8.5	13.8	21.8	59.8	2.8	36.7
1982	23.0	104.3	5.7	11.1	18.2	86.8	2.0	34.3

Barbados' trade with Caricom countries 1978-82 (Bds$ million)
Source: Barbados Statistical Service

(a) Which country exported the most goods to Barbados?

(b) Can you suggest at least one of the goods exported by that country?

(c) Can you suggest reasons for the decline in trade between Barbados and Guyana?

Regional bilateral agreements
These agreements include the Memorandum of Understanding between Barbados and Trinidad and Tobago, under which the terms of agreement regarding industrial development and trade are as follows.
Petroleum
(i) Trinidad will be given priority of supply for all Barbados-produced crude oil which is surplus to the requirements of Mobil Oil Barbados (National Petroleum Corporation).

(ii) Trintoc will supply National Petroleum of Barbados' requirements of reformate.

(iii) Trintoc and Lake Asphalt of Trinidad and Tobago Ltd have assumed the supply of 1.6 million gallons of asphalt for the road construction programme in Barbados.

Cement

A cement plant (Arawak Cement Company Ltd), situated in Barbados, using Barbados limestone and clay, has been set up on the following basis:

(i) joint shareholding between Trinidad and Tobago and Barbados, with Barbados holding most of the shares;

(ii) Trinidad and Tobago is to guarantee to take the surplus production of cement;

(iii) favourable arrangements for fuel surplus to the plant by the Government of Trinidad and Tobago;

(iv) loans will be mainly credit with the Government of Trinidad and Tobago, which will supply any shortfall in loan financing that may arise.

Iron and steel

(i) Both Governments agree that iron and steel are important to the economic development of the countries and agree to the maximum possible use of the products of the Trinidad and Tobago Steel Industry in development projects in both countries.

(ii) The two Governments agree that overseas offices such as the International Marketing Corporation (IMC) will, on request, be made available to each other on a mutually agreed basis.

Exchange of technology

The Government of Trinidad and Tobago will think about providing technical and financial assistance to Barbados in a petroleum exploration and development programme.

Transport and communication air services

The Governments of Trinidad and Tobago and Barbados agree to establish an All Cargo Air Services (Caricargo) with shareholding on a 50-50 basis.

(i) The service will be concerned with the most efficient movement of cargo in the Southern Caribbean and the most efficient use of cargo space to the area.

(ii) Operational date, August 1979.

(iii) There should be adequate protection from competition from other cargo services owned by either country.

(iv) Workers at certain levels should not lose their jobs as a result of the new air cargo service.

Joint tour operating company

The Governments agree that they should try to form a jointly owned tour operating company.

The terms of agreement regarding Trinidad and Tobago, Barbados and Antigua are as follows.

Transport and communication

(i) Assistance for expansion and development for a new airport terminal and construction of an airstrip on Barbados.

(ii) Antigua is committed to the principle of BWIA/TTAC as the regional carrier and to the rationalisation of air services in the Caribbean.

That on request the Government of Antigua would transfer to TTAC the route rights now enjoyed by BWIA. That LIAT headquarters in Antigua be expanded in order to service BWIA/TTAC.

(iii) Recommendation to be made that upon attainment of independence by Antigua, TTAC be permitted to use Antigua's International Route Rights.

(iv) Antigua indicated a desire to participate in the All Cargo Air Service Company and the Joint Tour Operating Company established between Trinidad and Tobago and Barbados.

PROBLEMS AFFECTING REGIONAL TRADE

There are many problems affecting the development of regional trade. One such factor is the problem of intra-regional transportation. In this regard we mean inadequate air and sea-port facilities, irregular, unreliable and inefficient air cargo and shipping services. Another factor, or set of factors, is that in many territories, roads, buildings (warehouse facilities), electrical and water supplies have not kept pace with the needs of the region.

Bureaucracy and government regulations are another set of factors affecting trade. For example, while containerisation has been welcomed in the region we find that government regulations have tended to reduce its effectiveness and to increase its cost of operation. Government regulations in terms of consumption duties, import licensing, tariffs, administrative mechanisms and dual exchange rates have all tended to reduce and hinder the development of regional trade. The most recent example of how government action affects regional trade was seen in the introduction of a dual exchange rate by Jamaica and the resultant reactions of the Government of Barbados, which caused its currency to float against Jamaica's, the Governments of Trinidad and Tobago and Antigua, which introduced import licences on all Caricom goods.

Violation of the rules-of-origin agreement by businessmen who import cheap garments from extra-regional sources and then sell them regionally is another problem facing regional trade. Other factors include the problems of productivity, pricing and marketing, which come under the heading of management.

Can you think of any other problem(s) which might affect regional trade? Can you think of some possible solutions to the problems?

THE CARICOM MULTILATERAL CLEARING FACILITY (CMCF)

The CMCF is a multilateral payments arrangement established in 1977 as a successor to the Intra-Regional Payments Scheme, which operated entirely on a bilateral basis. The objectives of the facility are:

(i) to facilitate settlement on a multilateral basis of eligible transactions between participating countries;
(ii) to promote the use of currencies of members in settling eligible transactions between the individual countries, thereby economising on the use of foreign exchange;
(iii) to promote monetary cooperation among the participants and close relations between their banking systems, thereby contributing to the expansion of trade and economic activity within Caricom.

The facility administered a US$100 million line-of-credit made available by the Government of Trinidad and Tobago. The line-of-credit works somewhat like an overdraft account. Its distribution among participants can be seen in the table below. (The figures show the direction of manifests.) Settlements, which amounted to reducing or eliminating the overdraft, occurred on 15 June and 15 December, provided that

| Participants | Extended | |
	By facility	To facility
Barbados	14.0	—
Belize	12.0	—
ECCA	20.0	—
Guyana	25.0	—
Jamaica	23.0	—
Trinidad and Tobago	6.0	—
Total	100.0	100.0

Line-of-credit administered by the CMCF (US$ million)

224

participants had not exceeded their credit limit. Individual participants were required to effect immediate settlement to the agent for any amount above their credit limit. However, on the date on which full payment was due participants had the option of settling a minimum of 50 per cent of their outstanding indebtedness. A concessional rate of interest was charged on debit balances. The interest was apportioned between the facility, to cover operational and other expenses, and participants with credit balances.

COUNTERTRADE

What exactly is countertrade and how can Caricom benefit from it? Essentially, countertrade involves the exchange of goods or services without the use of currency. It is a form of international trade where a party agrees to sell goods to a second party and simultaneously agrees to purchase other goods from the second party in a parallel transaction. Put another way, countertrade is the linking of purchases of foreign goods and services to exports of domestic goods by contract, which fully or partially offset, or sometimes exceed, the value of imported goods. For example, Jamaica agrees to supply the U.S.A. with bauxite in exchange for cars. Guyana agrees with Dominica to exchange rice for soap.

There are four basic forms of countertrade.

Barter This is straightforward exchange of goods and services between contracting parties. Usually no currency is involved and a single contract governs the entire transaction.

Compensation (buy back) This type of arrangement is generally used to sell machinery, equipment or technology. The seller of the equipment agrees to receive a portion of his payment in cash and the balance in the product produced by that equipment. Example A leases land from B to grow tomatoes, B being paid in tomatoes.

Counter-purchase In this type of agreement one party agrees to sell goods to another and the other agrees to purchase goods from the first party. They agree to sell each other products or services with some balancing value.

Switch Here trade is based on the multilateral use of bilateral clearing currencies. The clearing accounts are not directly convertible into cash but represent purchasing power for goods manufactured in the countries subscribing to the clearing agreement.

With a formalised system of countertrade regime, Caricom countries would stand to benefit for three main reasons:

(a) it would eliminate the need for hard foreign currency to finance settlements of intra-regional trade;

225

(b) it would commit Caricom member states to purchase from each other;

(c) with each member state, and ultimately within Caricom itself, it would foster closer ties between importers and exporters.

International agreements and agencies

THE EEC

The European Community, sometimes called the Common Market or the EEC, consists of nine European countries that have decided to work together towards economic and political unity. In 1951 Belgium, France, Germany, Italy, Luxemburg and the Netherlands decided to set up the European Coal and Steel Community with common institutions and rules. In 1958 two treaties came into being, setting up the European Economic Community and the European Atomic Energy Community (Euratons). Denmark, Ireland and the United Kingdom later joined the Community in 1973, followed by Greece in 1981. Today the EEC is the world's largest trader and the major importer of goods from the less developed countries.

The major aims of the EEC

Free movement of goods

The EEC has a customs union covering the exchange of all goods. The prohibition of customs duties on exports and imports between member states, and the adoption of a common external tariff in relation to third countries has been established.

Free movements of persons

Free movements of workers between member states. Workers may seek employment anywhere in the community, though governments retain the right, in some cases, to restrict free movement of labour. Nationals of member states enjoy equal treatment in every important field relating to employment, including matters relating to taxation, social insurance and dependants. Medical treatment on the same basis as that received by nationals is also available.

Free movement of capital

This is provided for in the treaty to achieve full economic and monetary union.

Approximation of fiscal policy

From 1st January 1973 a simple Value Added Tax system was applied throughout the six original member countries, and applied throughout the new members from 1st April 1973.

Free movement of services
The Right of Establishment is the right to engage in business and supply services anywhere in the community.

A common agricultural policy
(a) common market for all agricultural products;
(b) support buying to ensure that prices do not fall below agreed levels;
(c) a system of protective levies on agricultural imports from Third World Countries;
(d) the rationalisation of community agriculture.

THE ACP

The ACP is an association of 53 states of Africa, the Caribbean and the Pacific. These states are also associated with the EEC through the historical (former colonies) and trading links. The ACP are all developing countries with common problems, thus they have united to negotiate collectively with the EEC. ACP institutions are (i) the Council of Ministers, (ii) the Committee of Ambassadors, and (iii) the Secretariat.

THE LOMÉ CONVENTION

This is a contractual agreement between the EEC and the ACP states. The Convention was signed on 28th February 1977 in Lomé, capital of the Republic of Togo, after eighteen months of negotiation and more than one hundred and eighty meetings. Trade provisions came into force on 1st July 1975 and the Convention became fully operational on 1st April 1976. It expired in February 1980 but negotiations for a second agreement began in late 1978 and were completed in July 1979.

The main provisions of the Lomé Convention are:
(i) duty-free access, without reciprocity, to the European market, for goods exported from the ACP states;
(ii) a stabilisation fund to assist the ACP states in event of reductions in earnings they derive from the export of certain of their most important basic products;
(iii) financial and technical cooperation;
(iv) facilities for commercial promotions;
(v) industrial cooperation;
(vi) a commitment by the EEC to purchase specified quantities of ACP sugar;
(vii) provisions relating to the establishment of services, payments and capital movements to ensure non-discriminatory treatment of any ACP companies, firms and nationals;
(viii) the ACP-EEC institutions (Council of Ministers, Consultative Assembly) to provide for the joint management of the terms of the Lomé Convention.

Benefits of the Lomé agreement to the Caribbean
(a) Free trade with the EEC.
(b) A guaranteed market and price for sugar.
(c) Special arrangements for rum and bananas.
(d) Opportunities for trade in non-traditional goods, stimulation of investment, transferring of know-how and promotion of trade.
(e) Industrial and technical cooperation.
(f) Financing and the European Development Bank.
(g) Help from the Centre for Industrial Development in Brussels.

INTER-AMERICAN DEVELOPMENT BANK
The Inter-American Development Bank was founded in 1959 to promote the individual and collective development of member countries through the financing of economic and social development projects and the provision of technical assistance and help to implement the objectives of the Inter-American System.

The Activities of the IADB
(a) Ordinary capital resources. Loans are made to governments and to public and private bodies for specific economic projects. They are repayable in the currencies lent and their terms range from 10 to 25 years.
(b) Funds for special operations. The fund enables the bank to make loans for economic and social projects, the circumstances of which call for special treatment, such as lower interest rates and longer repayment terms than those applied to loans from the ordinary resources, and possibility of repayments in whole or part in local currency.
(c) Other funds. Funds are available for special assistance to Latin America, outside the above funds, e.g. Social Progress Trust Fund.
(d) Bond issues and loans.

OPEC
The Organisation of Petroleum Exporting Countries is a price fixing association (ring) of oil exporting countries. These countries have joined together to fix oil prices and so curtail competition among oil producing states. The aim of the organisation, which was founded in 1960, is to unify and coordinate members' petroleum policies and to safeguard their interests generally.

The members of OPEC are: Algeria, Ecuador, Gabon, Saudia Arabia, United Arab Emirates, Venezuela.

228

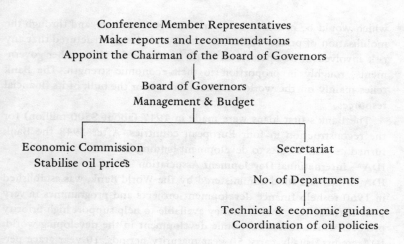

Conference Member Representatives
Make reports and recommendations
Appoint the Chairman of the Board of Governors

Board of Governors
Management & Budget

Economic Commission
Stabilise oil prices

Secretariat

No. of Departments

Technical & economic guidance
Coordination of oil policies

Organisation of OPEC

OPEC special fund

On January 28, 1976, in Paris, OPEC established a special fund to provide financial assistance to developing countries (other than their members) on concessionary terms. In particular, the fund's resources may be utilised in the following operations:

(a) providing loans to finance balance of payments deficits;
(b) providing loans to finance development projects and programmes;
(c) covering contributions which the contributing parties may make to international development agencies whose operations are directed to benefit developing countries.

THE WORLD BANK

Realising the need for international cooperative arrangements to deal with monetary and financial problems in the post-war world, the forty-four allied nations convened the United Nations Monetary and Financial Conference at Bretton Woods, New Hampshire, U.S.A. in July 1944. This conference drew up the Articles of Agreement (Charter) for two international financial institutions, (i) The International Monetary Fund (IMF) and (ii) The International Bank for Reconstruction and Development (World Bank). The Articles of Agreement came into force on December 27, 1945 when twenty-eight nations signed them in Washington D.C. The Bank began operations on June 25, 1946.

The Bank was created to make or guarantee loans for productive reconstruction and development projects, both from its own capital, which would be provided by its member governments, and through the mobilisation of private capital. Its share capital is so structured that any risk involved in its operations would be shared by all member governments, roughly in proportion to their economic strength. The Bank relies mainly on the world's capital markets for the bulk of its financial resources.

The Bank's first loans were made in 1947 (about $500 million) for the reconstruction in four European countries. After 1948 the Bank turned its main efforts to development lending.

IDA — International Development Association

IDA, which is a fund administered by the World Bank, was established in 1960 to help finance development projects and programmes in very poor nations. IDA makes money available to help support high-priority projects which foster economic development in the developing world. IDA credits usually carry 50 year maturity periods, 10 year grace periods before repayments of principal begins, and no interest, but an annual service charge of 75% on the disbursed portion of each credit, which is intended to cover administrative costs. IDA credits are designed to assist those very poor developing countries which cannot afford to borrow money on World Bank terms. IDA supports projects to develop agriculture, improve education, increase electric power output, expand industry, and create better urban facilities, etc. It also provides technical assistance, and occasionally makes money available for the purchase of imports not related to specific projects.

The main function of IDA is to provide foreign exchange and to provide it on terms that really poor developing countries can afford to accept. IDA lends only to governments.

IFC — International Finance Corporation

The International Finance Corporation (IFC) was established in 1956, and is the member of the World Bank Group that encourages the growth of productive private enterprise in the developing countries.

Membership of IFC is open to all governments which are members of the World Bank. The Corporation encourages private enterprise in the developing countries, principally by itself investing in projects that either establish new businesses, or expand, modernise or diversify existing businesses. IFC can, apart from making its own investments, recruit capital from other sources, local and foreign and obtain managerial and technical support for a project. IFC can offer other resources to local and foreign entrepreneurs, sponsors, technical partners and similar investors associated with its projects, in that it has at its disposal knowledge on financial, legal, technical and related aspects of private enterprise in developing countries.

IFC considers investment proposals from two points of view:
(a) that of an investment banker;
(b) that of a development institution.

Every project in which IFC invests should meet three basic conditions, (i) it should have profit earnings prospects; (ii) it should be beneficial to the economy of the country; (iii) local investors should be able to participate in the project, at the outset or later. Other conditions: (iv) the funds needed are not available on reasonable terms from private sources; (v) the financial plan for the project is realistic; (vi) there is a market for the product or service; (vii) management is capable and experienced; and (viii) the sponsor of the project has a substantial shareholding in the enterprise.

IFC is prepared to support joint ventures between private enterprise and a government. It will invest in a project only when there is no objection on the part of the government. It is always ready, if asked, to advise member governments upon policy relating to private investment.

IFC activities include investment in manufacturing, agriculture, tourism and other areas of investment.

IMF — THE INTERNATIONAL MONETARY FUND

The International Monetary Fund (IMF) which has been the chief organisation in international monetary and financial matters for the past three decades, originated from the Bretton Woods Agreement in 1944. The aims of the IMF are:
(a) to promote international monetary cooperation;
(b) to facilitate the growth of world trade and thereby the promotion of high levels of employment and real income;
(c) to promote exchange stability by maintaining orderly exchange arrangements among members and avoiding competitive depreciation;
(d) to establish a multilateral system of current payments and eliminate exchange restrictions;
(e) to make its resources available to members, under adequate safeguards, thus providing members with opportunity to correct maladjustments in their balance of payments without resorting to measures destructive to national or international prosperity.

The IMF is not and has never been a development institution. It is designed to provide medium term conditional finance to meet temporary balance of payments problems. The IMF does not disburse long-term concessional funds for development or for basic structural adjustments. IMF credit is of a revolving character and is available to all members, regardless of development status, which accords with the Fund's essentially monetary role. In recent years, the IMF has been modified in that a number of special facilities particularly beneficial to developing countries has been instituted. In 1952, stand-by arrangements were introduced allowing members to draw up to a specific amount within a fixed period of time. There must be close consultation during the life of the stand-by. This requirement enables the IMF to refuse an instalment of credit if agreed policies were not adhered to.

The amount that countries may draw (borrow) is dependent on their quotas (subscriptions) which determine members' rights and obligations in the IMF. They determine not only access but contributions to the Fund credit and voting power as well.

Questions

1   Outline the problems of development facing the Caribbean.
2   Define dualism, development, unemployment, migration, birth rate, industrialisation.
3   How has increasing population growth affected economic development in the Caribbean?
4   Make a list of different agencies which give aid and assistance to developing countries and write a brief note on each.
5   What is countertrade? How can countertrade help to increase regional trade?
6   What is a bilateral agreement? How can bilateral agreements increase regional trade?

27 The computer

The computer may be considered to be the most wonderful of all inventions. It has made the 'space age' possible by guiding space ships out of the earth's orbit into the far reaches of space and subsequently back to earth. It operates automated manufacturing systems. It makes possible the transmission of millions of dollars thousands of miles in a few seconds. It is used to carry out medical research to find new cures for disease and for innumerable other applications. Indeed, the computer is man's modern 'genie'.

We are all aware of the many uses of the computer, but how many of us know what a computer is? A computer is a device which accepts information (data), processes it and supplies results. The basic activities of a computer involve:

(a) accepting instructions that tell it how to operate;
(b) receiving data from one or more sources;
(c) processing data according to the instructions put into it;
(d) storing data (remembering) on a temporary or permanent basis; and
(e) sending data (information) to devices that display the data for an operator to read (TV screen or monitor), or to instruments which in turn control other equipment, such as a printer or cassette player.

One can therefore say that a computer is a device which manages data and information.

Types of computer

There are three basic varieties of computer.

1 **Mainframe computers** These are the largest of the computer family, both in size and in their extensive memory capacity.
2 **Micro-computers (also called personal computers)** These are the smallest of the computer family and may be seen on desks or table-

233

tops, in homes, schools and offices. Their memory (storage) capacity is small.

3   **The mini-computer** There is no clear separation between mini-computer and micro-computer. However, mini-computers tend to be larger than micro-computers in electronic capacity and certain other technical ways which enable them to operate faster than the micro-computers.

How a computer works

A basic computer system is composed of input units, which make data available to the processor unit, the processor unit, which stores data and processes that stored data, and output units, from which the results of the processing are obtained.

To get a computer to perform, it is necessary to give it instructions. Groups of instructions that guide computer operations are called programs. The programs are put into the random access memory (RAM) of the computer: (a) by being typed on a keyboard; (b) by means of magnetic tape in a cassette or on a disk; (c) by a combination of (a) and (b). Information stored on an audio cassette is fed into the computer via a cassette recorder. Most computers have a built-in memory system — read only memory (ROM), which is built into the computer by the manufacturers.

A complete computer system consists of:

(a) a keyboard and central processing unit,

(b) a video monitor,

(c) a cassette recorder and tape, or disk drive and disk,

(d) a printer, and

(e) a power module.

Use of computers in commerce and industry

There are five main areas of computer use in business. These are:

1   **As an aid to management** The computer allows very large volumes of data to be processed very quickly. Thus information can speedily be made available to management allowing rapid decisions to be made. The computer is also very accurate, given the right information. This helps management to make correct decisions and allows management by exception to occur. The latter process needs fast reporting to be effective and can be practised with a high degree of success with the aid of a computer. Management by exception

requires that only matters involving exceptional circumstances need be reported to management for attention.

2 **Control by computer** The computer is used to supervise the operations of controlling devices in large-scale continuous production, such as oil, chemical or textile production. Computers are also used to control space flights and monitor patients in hospital.

3 **Computerised research and design** Computers can be used by the research and development sector of business to test new designs and applications, for example aspects can be altered and the computer can quickly predict the effect of the various alterations. It can also be used in the standardisation of procedures.

4 **Computerised information systems** This is one of the main uses of the computer today, for example airlines use the computer for bookings.

5 **Computerised clerical operations** There are several applications of computerised clerical operations, for example wage and salary administration in large firms and credit and debit transfers in banks.

A brief history of computers

The ancestor of the present-day computer was the abacus, which was used in China, India and Japan for thousands of years and is still in widespread use. However, it is only recently that computer-like mechanical devices have been invented. The first such device to be called a computer was developed by a British mathematician, Charles Babbage, in 1812. This machine computed tables of mathematical functions. Babbage's principle of sequential control formed the basis for the development of Mark I, a machine developed by Dr Howard Aitken of Harvard University in 1944. This computer used the technique of opening and closing electro-magnetic relay switches to do its counting.

Dr John von Neumann in 1945 developed the first computer with a memory and he further suggested the use of binary numbers instead of decimal numbers in order to achieve greater power at less expense. Then in 1946 the first computer using vacuum tubes in its internal operation was perfected. It was called the ENIAC — Electronic Numerical Integrator and Computer. It took a small army of technicians to operate it.

The first computer to be mass-produced was the UNICAC, which was marketed by the Sperry Rand Corporation (1951). This machine employed a decimal and alphabetical system with magnetic tapes and a mercury-delay memory.

In 1953 IBM introduced the IBM 701, a machine with electrostatic memory. At about the same time, magnetic memory cores were developed, which led to faster processing and larger memories.

The next great step in the development of computers came with the use of semi-conductor transistors. These greatly reduced the size of computers while at the same time they increased operation speed and reliability. Magnetic tape and disk units were developed and used to store programs. The real breakthrough came with the invention of the integrated circuits developed by Fairchild in 1959. However it was the large-scale integrated circuit, a 'chip' developed in 1971, that really brought about the computer revolution. The 'chip', or micro-processor, is the brain of the modern computer. The LSI chips have led to much smaller computers with tremendous storage capacities, speed and accuracy.

Bibliography of references

1   *Leading Issues in Economic Development* (Second Edition) by Gerald Meier, Oxford University Press.
2   *Economic Development Challenges and Promise* Edited by S. Spiegelas and C.J. Welsh, Prentice-Hall Inc.
3   *The Structure Performance and Prospects of Central Banking in the Caribbean* by Clive Y. Thomas I.S.E.R. (U.W.I.).
4   *The Significance of Non-Bank Financial Intermediaries in the Caribbean* by Maurice A. Odle, I.S.E.R. (U.W.I.).
5   *Money and Banking in the East Caribbean Currency Area* by A. Wendell A. McClean, I.S.E.R. (U.W.I.).
6   *Monetary and Financial Arrangements in a Dependent Monetary Economy (A Study of British Guiana, 1945-1962)* by C.F. Thomas, I.S.E.R. (U.W.I.).
7   *The Lome Convention and a new International Economic Order* Edited by Frans A.M. Alting Von Geusan, J.F. Kennedy Institute Centre for International Studies.
8   *The European Community Facts and Figures.*
9   *Barbados National Bank Prospectus.*
10 *The E.E.C. and The Caribbean.*
11 *Change and Renewal in the Caribbean,* by W.G. Demas, CCC Publishing House, Barbados.
12 *A Businessman's Guide to the Caribbean Community* B.W.I.A. publication.
13 *The Caribbean Community — A Guide* Caribbean Community Secretariat.
14 *Caribbean Development Bank Basic Information* C.D.B. Publication.
15 *West Indian Social Problems* Edited by Malcolm Cross Columbus Publishers Ltd.
16 *West Indian Geography* by W. Williams Baily and P. Pemberton, Nelson & Sons Ltd.
17 *Exporting* by Taylor and Rutland, St. Paul's House, London.
18 *Business Administration* by L. Hall, MacDonald & Evans Ltd.
19 *The Structure of Business* by M.M. Lawton & J. Maguire, Hulton Educational Publications.
20 *An Outline of Monetary Theory* (2nd Edition) J.G. Houson, MacDonald & Evans Ltd.
21 *Economics of Public Finance* (2nd Edition) Edmund Seddon, MacDonald & Evans Ltd.
22 *The Europa Year Book 1978 Volume 1,* A World Survey.

Index